MANAGING OVERDUES

A How-To-Do-It Manual for Librarians

Edited by Patsy J. Hansel

HOW-TO-DO-IT MANUALS FOR LIBRARIANS

NUMBER 83

NEAL-SCHUMAN PUBLISHERS, INC.
New York, London

Published by Neal-Schuman Publishers, Inc.
100 Varick Street
New York, NY 10013

Library of Congress Cataloging-in-Publication Data

Managing overdues : a how-to-do-it manual for librarians / edited by
Patsy J. Hansel.
     p.   cm.—(How-to-do-it manuals for librarians ; no. 83)
   Includes bibliographical references.
   ISBN 1–55570–291–0
   1. Library overdues—United States. I. Hansel, Patsy.
II. Series: How-to-do-it manuals for Libaries ; no. 83.
Z712.M36 1998
025.1—dc21   98–16348
                                       CIP

CONTENTS

PREFACE

Dealing with the problem of books that are returned late, or never at all, is both time-consuming and costly. The cost of items that are actually lost is both obvious and easily documented. The cost of books sitting in closets or under beds or wherever overdue books reside until they are finally returned and made available to others is much more difficult to calculate.

As library managers we tend to avoid the overdues issue because we cannot "solve" the problem. No matter how efficient our systems are, a fair number of items will not come back when they are due, and a somewhat smaller number will never come back at all. Some of us consider the disappearance of thousands of painstakingly selected, carefully cataloged items a basic cost of doing business—which it definitely is. However, it is also a very real cost, one which when it becomes public rarely redounds to our credit in the media. It behooves all library managers to know the actual extent of the overdue problem in their libraries and to feel confident that they are using the most effective strategies to manage this problem. This is the only way that we can be ready to answer the tough questions when they are asked. *Managing Overdues: A How-To-Do-It Manual for Librarians* presents proven strategies you can incorporate to help you manage the overdues problem in your library.

Henry Dutcher's efforts to get long-overdue materials returned to the Springfield (Massachusetts) Public Library in 1995 was the impetus for a flurry of nationwide publicity about how libraries deal with people who don't return materials paid for with taxpayer dollars. While researching this "issue," many of the reporters for major papers—including *The New York Times*—called the American Library Association for background information. When I started receiving calls from these reporters, I learned that I was "The Expert" to whom ALA was directing them. My "expert" status derived from some research on overdues that Robert Burgin (a professor at North Carolina Central University's School of Library and Information Studies) and I had done in the 1980s.

Part I, "Long Overdue: New Methods for Retrieving Overdue Books," begins with Henry Dutcher, the Springfield, Massachusetts, librarian whose program started the nationwide publicity that eventually led to this book being written. Dutcher describes his experiences using the courts to get long-overdue items back. I urge you to pay particular attention to the way he managed to generate an excellent corresponding public relations program for his library.

Judy Fuss, systems administrator for the Williamsburg (Virginia) Regional Library, then details her success using an electronic notification system to speed up the return of overdue materials.

Amazingly, she not only lowered her overdues rate, but she also reduced the amount of staff time spent on overdues and the annual expenditures for supplies and postage related to overdues.

Next, two staff members from the Rowan Public Library (Salisbury, North Carolina)—Melody Moxley, administrative services manager, and Jeff Hall, operations manager—tell us how they used a credit bureau to help get overdue items back. Susan Swanton, director of the Gates Public Library (Rochester, New York), used a collection agency. Her description of using collection agencies for overdue books is followed by supplementary information from the American Collectors Association that should be of interest to librarians who have never considered this tactic.

Part II, "The Taxman and the Lottery: Using Setoff Programs to Collect Overdue Accounts," describes different approaches to using a state's setoff debt program for dealing with patrons who have long-term overdue items. Setoff debt programs allow debts to be paid from money that a state owes its citizens (e.g., income tax refunds or lottery winnings). They exist in many states, but libraries are not always eligible to use them, so you'll need to check to see if you can use this tactic in your state. Judy Fuss tells us how the Williamsburg Regional Library used this system. Sharon Winters (formerly support services manager for the Hampton (Virginia) Public Library, now deputy director for Support Services at the Pierce County Library District in Tacoma, Washington) describes how she used her local government apparatus to tap into a setoff debt program, and Susan M. Johns, systems/circulation librarian at the Axe Library (Pittsburg, Kansas), and professor of library science, Pittsburg State University, explains how a library that is a state agency uses a state setoff debt program. As one who has seen setoff debt programs make a tremendous difference, I encourage you to tap into these programs if you're eligible. If your state does not yet allow libraries to participate, I urge you to begin working with your state library association to amend the legislation so that you can.

Part III, "More about Managing Overdues," features Julie Walker's (assistant director, Athens [Georgia] Regional Library) update of the "do fines help reduce overdues" debate. Terry Prather's excellent selective bibliography on overdues concludes the book.

While dealing with overdue books and delinquent fines is a never-ending challenge, the techniques described in this book provide librarians with additional ammunition in the ongoing battle to be ever-more responsible stewards of public money.

Patsy J. Hansel, Director
Williamsburg Regional Library
Williamsburg, Virginia

INTRODUCTION

Interestingly, it is easier for us to ignore overdues now that most libraries are automated than it was back when we all had manual circulation systems. Back then (and now, for those of you still using manual systems), the reality of overdue items confronted us daily as hundreds—or thousands—of book cards filed in long wooden trays.

I still remember vividly the backroom of the first public library where I worked. The overdues clerk's desk was in front of a ten-foot work counter. Those wooden boxes were lined up by year on top of the counter, representing thousands of books that had been checked out of our library and never returned. You had only to dip into those boxes and pull up cards for books long disappeared to have your heart broken and your faith in humanity seriously damaged. Ours was a small library, and we all worked so hard to get a little more money in the book budget each year so that we could develop that elusive fabulous collection that is the goal of all true library supporters. Yet, the overdue card file grew as quickly as we could add books to the collection. To us, each card was a chess book, an expensive art book, an in-demand cookbook, or a popular novel that another user would have to wait—and wait—to read.

Some of us could go about our daily tasks, heedless of the growing monster in the backroom, but not Terry Bossley (now Terry Prather, the compiler of this book's bibliography). Terry was in charge of overdues in that small public library. She had to keep those files in order, adding new cards as they moved from being merely "overdue" (with some hope of being returned to the library) to being "long overdue" (gone; absolutely, irretrievably gone). It's easy for administrators to talk about "The Cost of Doing Business," but when you're a Terry Bossley, in charge of the dirty underbelly of the library business, you can't just ignore the problem. So, one day Terry asked (for about the hundredth time), "Isn't there *something* we can do about all these overdues?"

That was the day I got involved in researching the overdues problem. We enlisted the help of Robert Burgin (then a fellow public librarian, now a library educator) and surveyed North Carolina public libraries to find out just how bad the problem was and to find out if there were any libraries that seemed to be doing a better job of managing the problem so that the rest of us could replicate their success. After we completed the survey, we invited people to a few workshops around the state so they could hear about the survey results and listen to people whose libraries, according to the survey, seemed to be doing things right. I'll tell you more about what we found in this initial survey later, but first let me tell you that when we did a second survey, we added just one question: "Did you change anything as a result of the workshops?"

What we found was that if a library had changed anything related to overdues management—it didn't seem to matter what—that library did significantly better in getting materials returned than those libraries that didn't change anything. Herein lies my hope for you: that implementing one or more of the strategies in this manual will reduce your library's overdues problem.

ABOUT THE FOUR SURVEYS

THE FIRST SURVEY—1981

In the first survey, we surveyed only libraries in North Carolina. That survey showed that

1. Libraries that took offenders to court had significantly higher overdues than those that did not. We assumed, of course, that taking people to court was a result, not the cause, of having a high overdues rate.
2. The larger the population served, the higher the overdues rate; and
3. Libraries that sent out their overdues notices quickly (within two weeks of the book being due) had significantly lower overdues rates than libraries that sent out notices later.

None of the libraries surveyed had automated procedures.

THE SECOND SURVEY—1983

The 1983 survey included libraries outside of North Carolina. Results from those libraries were no different statistically from those in North Carolina, but we did get some new findings. Overdues rates were generally lower than they had been in the first survey, for both short-term and long-term overdues. We also made three other findings: libraries that restricted patrons with overdues from checking out more books got their books back faster; the few automated libraries that responded to our survey had lower overdues rates than nonautomated libraries; and our favorite finding—libraries that changed something after attending our 1982 workshops did significantly better at getting their books back than those who did not.

Based on the results from these two surveys, Burgin and I suggested some strategies that appear to be most successful in winning the war on overdues:

1. Automating circulation procedures;
2. Restricting those with overdues from checking out any more materials;
3. Taking the worst offenders to court;
4. Not charging fines;
5. Sending the first overdues notice within two weeks of the due date; and
6. Making the final notice a bill for the book.

THE THIRD SURVEY—1986

This was the survey that turned our little overdues business upside down. Based on that survey, nothing libraries did made a statistically significant difference in their overdues rate (with the possible exception of automation, but only one automated library responded). What was particularly disturbing was that there was no relationship between a library's 1983 and 1986 overdues rate that could be accounted for by a particular change in strategy. Since our goal was to find out how libraries could lower their overdues rate and thereby keep more library resources in circulation, we were disappointed.

However, even in the absence of statistically significant findings from our survey, we were not without our "gut response" conclusions based on more than five years of concentrated overdues work with many libraries of all sizes:

1. One was a suspicion that statistics from libraries using manual circulation systems were somewhat unreliable and thus the cause of some inconsistencies in data over the years.
2. Another of our beliefs was that the success of a procedure had as much to do with how efficiently it was implemented as with what the procedure was.
3. Finally, we felt that much of the strategies' success depended on the local situation—i.e., what worked in one community was not necessarily transferable to another community.

THE FOURTH SURVEY—1995

In preparing for this book, I decided to try one more survey, which I distributed via hard copy to all public libraries in Virginia and via the Internet to libraries across the country.

The return rate was abysmal. Libraries that filled out the form completely tended to be both very small and unautomated. When I queried automated libraries about incomplete responses or nonresponses, their answers were uniform: it isn't easy to get these numbers out of our computers. I pestered some of the larger libraries—wheedling, pleading, and calling in past favors—and was finally able to reach the conclusion that automation is a *huge* help in getting items returned.

My favorite information in this survey came from a very large library system in North Carolina that amazingly still had their information from the original 1981 survey. They had made no other changes to their overdues strategy. Their long-overdue rate in their unautomated days was two percent of all circulations. In 1992, when they fully automated circulation, that rate fell to 0.5 percent. If their two percent rate had continued into 1992, they would have lost 32,449 books that year, as opposed to the 8,814 they actually lost. That difference in overdues management, at a conservative rate of $20.00 per book, means the library saved more than $473,700 in one year. If that library suddenly had a $473,700 infusion into its operating budget, its managers would have been ecstatic. However, they weren't even aware of the "in-kind" contribution their automation system was making to their collection management until I happened to ask them for data.

Similarly, in the other six automated libraries from which I was able to get information, long-overdues rates ranged from 0.5 percent downwards. In comparison, the lowest average rate from the earlier surveys was 0.66 percent. I remember the days when library directors tried to obtain automation funds by telling funders that automation would enable staff salary savings. I think by now we've all learned that automation does not necessarily reduce library staff needs, but it certainly does allow us to offer better service to our communities. What we can now claim, though, is that automation saves us huge amounts of money each year because it enables us to greatly reduce our losses from overdues.

MANAGING OVERDUES SAVES MILLIONS OF DOLLARS

If we assume that the surveys I did in the 1980s based on manual statistics provide a fairly accurate picture of the national overdues rate, we'd have a rounded-off average of 0.7 percent. If we also assume from my "quick and dirty" 1995 survey that the overdues rate in the largely automated 1990s is below 0.5 percent, perhaps 0.45 percent, we would have a reduction of 0.25 percent. In 1994, the last year for which I could get national public library circulation statistics from the National Center for Education Statistics, annual circulation for public libraries in the United States was 1,570,024,000. Using the pre-automated long-overdue rate of 0.7 percent, libraries would have lost 10,990,168 items that year. At $20 per item, that would have come to a national loss of $219,803,360. Using the automated libraries' average long-overdue rate of 0.4 percent and that same $20 per book, the loss would have been 6,280,096 items or $125,601,920. This means that the lower overdues rate that we are able to obtain with automation comes to a national annual savings of $94,201,440 of taxpayer money. If we had that amount added to LSTA each year, wouldn't we be pleased?

While my research and unscientific assumptions suggest that the overdues picture is much brighter than it was prior to automation, I am not suggesting that we can rest easy. Our libraries are still suffering unnecessary losses from long-overdue items, and there are procedures we can implement that will help us decrease these losses or obtain reimbursement for truly lost items. The chapters that follow provide techniques that, when properly implemented, should help your library significantly lower its overdue rate.

PART I:
LONG OVERDUE:
FOUR METHODS FOR
RETRIEVING OVERDUE BOOKS

1 PROSECUTE OFFENDERS

by Henry Dutcher

SPRINGFIELD CITY LIBRARY
SPRINGFIELD, MASSACHUSETTS

With over 900,000 volumes and a circulation approaching 1,000,000 a year, the Springfield City Library serves a diverse population of just over 150,000 city residents and more than 350,000 people regionally. The City Library is one unit of the Springfield Library and Museums Association, which encompasses four museums and the library system, with its main downtown building and eight neighborhood branches.

Although the Springfield Library and Museums Association receives approximately 60 percent of its funding from the city, it is a private, nonprofit organization. In addition to funding, the association receives certain benefits from the city, such as participation in the city retirement system and in the health and life insurance programs.

In 1989, I was employed by the City Library as a reference librarian. That year, because of a state and city budget crisis, the library's public funding was cut some 40 percent, which necessitated comparable levels of reductions in hours and staff. Because of these constraints, many library procedures that had been considered "routine" were drastically reduced. The pursuit of overdue materials was among those activities that were all but eliminated. We continued to send overdue and billing notices to patrons, but there was no follow-up. Thus, materials that were not returned, in spite of these mailings, were left unattended.

The mission of a public library is to make information accessible to everyone, but by 1995 there were 58,000 "lost" items throughout the library system. Because these long-overdue materials were not available to our patrons, we faced a very serious public service problem—one that could have financial repercussions, as well. Even some of our most supportive patrons were becoming frustrated by this situation and questioning our allowing it to continue. We certainly could not afford to jeopardize this traditional base of support.

When I was interviewed for my position, we discussed the need to actively address this serious backlog, and the materials recovery program began to take shape. A recent amnesty period had been unsuccessful and it seemed there were few other options available.

However, we did have one rather drastic weapon at our disposal. An obscure Massachusetts law allows for the prosecution of individuals who do not return library materials (see Figure 1.1). The statute calls for a minimum fine of $100 to a maximum fine of $500 per item. The administration was concerned that taking people to court for overdue books would create negative publicity, potentially damaging future fundraising efforts.

FIGURE 1.1 Massachusetts Statute

§ 99A. Libraries; theft of materials or property; destruction of records

Whoever willfully conceals on his person or among his belongings any library materials or property and removes said library materials or property, if the value of the property stolen exceeds two hundred and fifty dollars, shall be punished by imprisonment in the state prison for not more than five years, or by a fine of not less than one thousand nor more than twenty-five thousand dollars, or both; or, if the value of the property stolen does not exceed two hundred and fifty dollars, shall be punished by imprisonment in jail for not more than one year or by a fine of not less than one hundred nor more than one thousand dollars, or both, and ordered to pay the replacement value of such library materials or property, including all reasonable processing costs, as determined by the governing board of said library.

Any person who has properly charged out any library materials or property, and who, upon neglect to return the same within the time required and specified in the by-laws, rules or regulations of the library owning the property, after receiving notice from the librarian or other proper custodian of the property that the same is overdue, shall willfully fail to return the same within thirty days from the date of such notice shall pay a fine of not less than one hundred nor more than five hundred dollars and shall pay the replacement value of such library materials or property, including all reasonable processing costs, as determined by said governing board. Each piece of library property shall be considered a separate offense.

The giving of a false identification or fictitious name, address or place of employment with the intent to deceive, or borrowing or attempting to borrow any library material or property by: the use of a library card issued to another without the other's consent; the use of a library card knowing that it is revoked, canceled or expired; or, the use of a library card knowing that it is falsely made, counterfeit or materially altered shall be punished by a fine of not less than one hundred dollars nor more than one thousand dollars.

The willful alteration or destruction of library ownership records, electronic or catalog records retained apart from or applied directly to the library materials or property shall be punished by imprisonment in the state prison for not more than five years or by a fine of not less than one thousand nor more than twenty-five thousand dollars, or both, and shall pay the replacement value of such library materials or property, including all reasonable processing costs, as determined by the governing board having jurisdiction.

Added by St.1990, c. 61.

Our public relations department contacted other large libraries in the region to see if they had ever used a similar hard-line approach and what the results had been. We found that a few libraries had used collection agencies, and one had taken a single individual to court. However, most librarians expressed their concern about adverse public reaction to the prosecution of delinquent borrowers.

Nevertheless, I had a very strong sense that with a well-planned, well-executed publicity campaign, we could turn this potential negative into a very strong positive. We agreed upon three major themes as the foundation for our message to the public: 1) public service—the library could not meet the needs of the public without the missing materials, 2) responsible stewardship of the taxpayers' dollars, and 3) sound management practices—we could no longer tolerate these monetary losses.

To proceed, we needed the full cooperation of the district attorney's office. I first contacted an assistant district attorney I knew, but his initial reaction was not encouraging. He indicated that with all the drugs, murders, rapes and other "real crimes," he could not imagine the district attorney devoting resources to something like this. However, he gave me the name of the first assistant district attorney, Judy Zeprun Kalman, and wished me good luck. From the beginning, my reception with Judy was extremely positive. She was appalled at our situation and identified herself as an ardent reader and regular library patron, who had been inconvenienced herself by "lost" items. She assured me that she wanted to help but would need the approval of the district attorney. The very next day she called to say District Attorney William M. Bennett took less than thirty seconds to grant approval. His reaction was "do whatever it takes." With this hurdle behind us we were ready to proceed.

We decided to lay out our entire strategy to the public and inform them of our plans at least a month before any notices were sent. This would allow time for any negative reaction to surface. We also wanted to stress that we really wanted to reinstate the delinquent borrowers as library patrons in good standing—a goal we repeatedly emphasized throughout the campaign.

The media campaign started out routinely enough. Our publicist contacted the Springfield *Union News,* the local daily newspaper, early one afternoon and told them about our materials-recovery campaign and the possibility that patrons might actually be taken to court if they did not respond. The paper was so intrigued by this story that they sent a reporter over within the hour. We were quite pleased the next day when the piece ran as the lead story of the local news section.

The next day the books started to trickle back in, some of them a number of years overdue. Also, we received many phone calls from patrons anxiously inquiring if they had any unreturned materials on their records.

Meanwhile, the newspaper contacted us again for a follow-up story. To our delight, the story and color photo ran on the front page of the Springfield *Union News,* "above the fold."

The local radio and television stations were getting into the act as well, and over the next few days I was interviewed on almost all of them. It seemed that everyone wanted to do a story on our "scofflaws," as the press had dubbed them. More overdue materials poured in.

On the morning of the first newspaper article, the irreverent morning disc jockeys at a local rock radio station were having great fun with the story of the librarian intending to take library patrons to court. As a regular listener of the station, I called in and offered them an impromptu interview. That interview lasted five minutes; afterwards I found out from my wife that whenever I spoke, they played the *Dragnet* theme song behind my voice. After leaving the air, they quite innocently said just to let them know if there was anything they could do to help out. Little did they know just how pushy I could be.

That morning I informed my library director and the public relations staff of the radio station's offer. I spoke with them about my intention to solicit a live remote broadcast in the library designed to encourage patrons to return their lost items. A discussion ensued about the propriety of a rock station in the library, particularly these two somewhat controversial disc jockeys. My argument, the one that perhaps carried the most weight, was that none of the listeners would find offense in anything the disc jockeys said because they would already be regular listeners.

After a few days of negotiations with the radio station, they agreed to provide us, free of charge, a four-hour remote broadcast from our rotunda. During the time on the air, patrons returning overdue materials would not have to pay fines.

What great fun for the whole library! Without any prodding, a number of staff members volunteered to be at the library by 6 A.M. to help. Over the next four hours, morale in the library reached a five-year high, in spite of the fact that we were taking the ribbing of a lifetime. The disc jockeys entertained everyone—the adventurous patrons with their overdue books, the listeners, and the staff—with just about every library joke in the book. The highlight of the morning was the contest to find out who could bring back the longest overdue book. We had already seen books more than ten years overdue and never expected to see anything much older than that. So, when the *Book of Wireless* appeared, seventy-three years overdue, we were as amazed as the disc jockeys who had found just the entertainment angle they were looking for. The person was returning the book for his grandfather and, needless to say, he won the prize.

With the next event our story developed a life of its own. The local Associated Press reporter contacted us for a story on our campaign; we were delighted, of course. After a lengthy interview and photo session, he assured us that the story would receive at least regional coverage and that a Saturday release was planned. On Monday, when we still had not seen the piece, the library publicist called the reporter and was told he was in the middle of dealing with the fact that the piece had just been released in A.P.'s National Digest, a listing for editors of the day's top feature stories. The flood gates broke open.

That Monday I could hardly set the phone down before it rang again.

The first phone call was from a small radio station in Manhattan, Kansas; they just wanted an interview for their morning news program. I thought it a little odd, but I gladly obliged. From there, it just got crazier and crazier. Over the course of the day, I spoke to the National Mutual Radio Service, CNN Radio, CBS radio's Osgood Files, and NBC radio.

Then, near the end of the day, CNN Television News called to ask if they could drive up from New York the following day to do a feature story on us. The story aired repeatedly over the next several days. In fact, one of our trustees saw it while vacationing in Italy.

We also found out that based on the Associated Press wire release we appeared in close to one hundred newspapers around the country that week, including the *Philadelphia Inquirer, Washington Times, Boston Globe,* and most amazing of all, the Sunday edition of the *New York Times.*

Back at the library we were coping with book drop after book drop loaded with materials, some more than ten years overdue. And we had yet to contact a delinquent patron directly.

For me, the most surprising thing was the way old friends and acquaintances began to surface. One afternoon as I sat at my desk preparing for a staff meeting, the phone rang. I answered and a vaguely familiar voice asked, "Is this the Henry Dutcher from Fredonia State?" To my amazement, I found myself speaking with a former fiancée. That fifteen-minute conversation helped to resolve issues that were more than eighteen years old.

None of us imagined that our media campaign would generate such a tremendous response. But, regardless of how much fun or how productive that was, there was real work to be done. At the beginning of our program, we received a printout of the worst offenders: those individuals with more than $200 worth of overdue items. That list had almost four hundred names, and those were the people we planned to target with our mailings. We had decided that going after anyone with materials worth less than $200 would not be cost effective. Thousands of patrons fell into this category, and the cost of pursuing them individually would have been prohibitive. Furthermore, the publicity alone seemed to be taking care of a good portion of the lesser offenders, and as we got closer and closer to court dates, we expected even more materials to come in.

A letter (Figure 1.2) was created to inform the patrons of our intention to go after the materials they still possessed. The letter informed them of the fines or replacement costs required to take care of their situations. It also outlined the provision of the Massachusetts General Laws (G.L. Chap. 266, Sec. 99A) that we were using to pursue them. There is a significant Latino population in this area, so the letter was produced in Spanish as well.

FIGURE 1.2 Letter to Library Patron with Overdue Materials

SPRINGFIELD CITY LIBRARY
220 State Street, Springfield, MA 01103

Dear Library User:

This is your last notice that materials charged to you are overdue and need to be returned.

According to our records, the library material listed on the enclosed notice was charged to your card by you and never returned to the library. It is unfortunate that you did not take advantage of our recent amnesty period because we must now take other steps to retrieve this material.

Keeping library property is a criminal violation of the law printed below—Massachusetts Law, Chapter 266, Section 99A.*

If, for whatever reason, you cannot return the material you borrowed, you will be charged replacement costs and processing fees. If you return these materials, you will not be charged the replacement cost or processing fees. **However, even if you return the material, you will need to pay a maximum fine of $3 per item ($10 per item for videos and a few other unique items) to clear your record.** Please visit any library location with the material and fines or replacement/processing fees, in order to clear your record. Enclosed is a listing of hours, locations and phone numbers for the branches.

By promptly returning the items charged to you, along with the payment of the maximum fine, or the replacement costs for those items, you will once again become a borrower in good standing.

It is the policy of the Springfield City Library not to charge late fines for patrons 11 years of age and under, or for patrons 62 years of age and older. However, the library will charge replacement costs and processing fees for all unreturned materials regardless of a patron's age.

The Springfield City Library provides important information and service to all segments of the community. With current financial conditions it is very difficult to replace unreturned items and to purchase new materials. When library items are not returned, the whole community suffers.

If by _____ this matter has not been resolved we will be forced to pursue other collection methods which may include legal action.

*Chapter 266 section 99A. Libraries; theft of materials or property; destruction of records
Any person who has properly charged out any library materials or property, and who, upon neglect to return the same within the time required and specified in the by-laws, rules or regulations of the library owning the property, after receiving notice from the librarian or other proper custodian of the property that the same is overdue, shall willfully fail to return the same within thirty days from the date of such notice shall pay a fine of not less than one hundred dollars nor more than five hundred dollars and shall pay the replacement value of such library materials or property, including all reasonable processing costs, as determined by said governing board. Each piece of library property shall be considered a separate offense.

For a juvenile or young adult patron we sent an accompanying letter to the parents (Figure 1.3) indicating that their child was delinquent. Because we have a strong commitment to confidentiality, we told the parents the number of items and the replacement value but never which items were charged out to their child.

FIGURE 1.3 Letter to Parents of Minor with Overdue Materials

Under separate cover your son/daughter was recently informed of substantial overdues/ fines. State confidentiality laws and the Library Bill of Rights require us to send notices containing any information which would divulge what materials a patron has charged out only to that patron. We felt you would wish to be notified about your son/daughter's situation. The total charges are _____ dollars for _____ items. We would appreciate your assistance in settling this matter.

All mailings to the adult patrons included a listing of the items they still had out, the replacement cost, a 50-percent-off-fines coupon (Figure 1.4), plus a listing of the library's hours. The coupon was good for one week after receipt of the letter and could be used only for fines on returned items, not for replacement costs. However, during the entire program only two coupons were used.

FIGURE 1.4 Discount Coupon

SPRINGFIELD CITY LIBRARY
220 State Street, Springfield, MA 01103

DISCOUNT COUPON
**Return your materials (with this coupon) by _____
and receive a 50% discount on your fines.**
Does not apply to replacement costs or processing fees.

The Massachusetts statute required that all mailings be sent certified. The first assistant district attorney recommended that the mailings be sent return receipt so we would have proof that the patron received the notice.

Late in May, we sent our first mailing, to approximately fifty people who had more than $400 worth of materials overdue. We quickly realized that this type of mailing was not going to work for us. Only two people out of the fifty actually signed for their own notices. Upon consultation with the post office, we realized that our mailings needed to include the restricted-delivery option. This raised our cost per item from $2.55 to $5.52, but it was necessary in order to have proof in the courts that the individual named had actually received the letter. Also, because some of the cases were more than six years old, more than half of the letters were returned because addresses were out-of-date. We re-sent eighteen letters with this new restricted-delivery option, but still only received notification that five had been signed for by the targeted individuals. The problems of out-of-date addresses and inability to reach the right person continued throughout the program.

With each step of the campaign, we received additional publicity, and with each news article or radio and television report, we received more and more materials back. We quickly realized that the public relations campaign was providing us with the best results. Over the course of the summer, we continued to send out our mailings in groups of twenty or thirty letters, getting fewer than ten signed receipts from the addressees. Each mailing had its own deadline, and the letter stated when the next step would be taken to gather materials if they were not voluntarily returned.

As required by the Massachusetts statute, we gave everyone thirty days to respond. During this thirty-day period, usually two or three people from each mailing would come in to settle with us, almost always by returning the items. Seldom did anyone pay the replacement costs. Although we never asked why the patron had not come in until that point, some of the excuses we heard were quite amazing: "Oh, I've been meaning to, I've been meaning to . . . " about items that were four and five years overdue. We heard about one set of items sitting in a box in the closet for the past six years. Another batch of materials was "out of town"—we're still not sure if the patron was trying to tell us that the materials were on a vacation or some other trip.

When the thirty-day period was up on the first mailing, we took our first five names to the district attorney. Again, in our efforts to handle this as courteously as possible, the district attorney arranged with the district court clerk's office to schedule show cause hearings for these patrons. Show cause hearings allow individuals to show some reason why a criminal complaint should not be brought against them. We hoped that perhaps another chance, but in a legal setting, would show that we really meant business. The patrons could then take care of the matter without any further court costs or legal entanglements.

Our first show cause hearing almost brought the entire campaign to a crashing halt. Much to our amazement, the clerk magistrate assigned to administer the hearing obviously did not agree with our campaign. He felt that the campaign was using valuable court resources for a matter that clearly did not belong with crimes such as assault or burglary. He quickly dismissed the first patron's case, saying that the individual did not show a *willful* disregard for returning the materials, although those materials were more than four years overdue and the person readily admitted that she had not returned them. Needless to say, both the first assistant district attorney and I were shocked. We managed to get a continuance with the second patron. Since the other three individuals did not show up, the clerk magistrate had no recourse but to issue the complaints and a summons to appear in district court, thus salvaging our campaign to that point. From then on, the first assistant district attorney had the cases placed on the daily court list for arraignment and conference, thereby preventing further delay at the clerk-magistrate level.

Again, only two people showed up during the next group's scheduled arraignments. Both individuals were granted a continuance, as they both expressed a desire to settle the matter with us. Since then, one has started to make restitution. I still had not heard from the other person as late as a month before his next court date. The others had arrest warrants issued against them for failure to appear in court. Throughout late summer and early fall, we continued to alternate between sending out mailings and going to court with those whose deadlines had passed.

These court appearances were something to behold. On one occasion, I sat through several hours of drunk drivers, domestic assaults, and similar cases until the library patrons were called forward. One of the local television stations was there to film the entire process. Two individuals were arraigned together and both readily admitted they had charged out the materials. One of them, a young man, quite blatantly indicated that he just never expected that we would really come after him and he had planned to keep the materials. The other one carried her books into court. To this day we cannot understand why she did not return them to the library, rather than let it get to a court appearance. Both patrons pleaded no contest and were assessed a victim witness fee of $30.

That same morning, a man was called up and down on appearances for a number of problems, ranging from drunk driving to driving without a license or registration, etc. As I was leaving the court to speak with the television reporter, this gentleman opened the door for me and said encouragingly, "Way to go." Even with all of his problems, he understood the ethics of returning library materials.

Both patrons were asked to appear with the television crew to answer questions. The young woman vehemently declined. The young man said, "Hey, cool." In the interview with our local television reporter, he reiterated that he never believed the library would really come after him and, indeed, he had had every intention of keeping the CDs that he had borrowed. He stated this on camera with no remorse and then asked when he would be on TV. We felt his cockiness was one of our best public relations tools. We knew many people would not want to be identified with his attitude and would do whatever they could to get their materials back. Indeed, the next few days were some of our most productive.

As the cycle of court appearances, mailings, and publicity continued, it was clear that we were reaching a point of diminishing returns and the campaign was finding its natural end. To date six people have been issued arrest warrants. To my knowledge, only one of them has been picked up. The sheriff has made it clear that finding them is not a priority; they will just be picked up the first time they come in contact with the police.

The time had come to put into effect our long-term strategy for materials recovery. We do not intend to let the problem get out of hand again. We have recently contracted with a collection agency to pursue all current overdues. We will continue to send out overdue and billing notices in house, but will rely on the collection agency if the materials are not returned.

So, was it all worth it? Unquestionably! In concrete terms, we only received approximately 6,300 items valued at approximately $220,000, a recovery rate of just over 10 percent. Because the materials were many years overdue and many borrowers had moved, some people questioned whether it was worth the effort to pursue any of them. But the results extend well beyond those figures. First, we did manage to recover more than 10 percent of the outstanding materials. Second, we received invaluable publicity, all of it positive. A letter to the editor (Figure 1.5) printed in the Springfield *Union News* on May 2, 1995, is a perfect example of the public sentiment about our program. Third, our current overdues have been reduced by almost one third. If that trend continues, it will mean a savings of almost $60,000 a year, plus enhancement of public service by making those materials available for use.

Throughout the campaign, our goal was to reverse the trend of increasing losses, and the media attention we received seems to have accomplished this. In fact, several neighboring suburban libraries have reported a decrease in overdues as a result of our efforts.

What were our costs? As you can see (Figure 1.6), most of the outlay was for staff time. It should be noted that I handled all aspects of the campaign myself in order to avoid losing anyone in the legal system. Also, since patron records are confidential and there was intense media interest in these particular records, I felt it was best to limit access to them. This commitment required a considerable amount of

---

FIGURE 1.5 Letter to the Editor, *Union News*, May 2, 1995.

Throw book at library thieves

The April 28 article in your paper regarding library thefts really angered me. First, the city has under-funded the libraries, thus making it impossible for them to remain open on a daily basis.

Many of the branches are open for fewer than 20 hours per week. This I feel is a deterrent to the city's well-being.

Furthermore, the same article pointed out a complete disrespect to all other library patrons. In my view, these offenders cause a great injustice to those in the community who wish to better themselves through art, literature, music, and the other resources the library has to offer.

How can we as citizens, expect the city to provide a better and more accessible library if certain individuals take improper advantage of our public resources?

Let's hope that through the legal actions now being taken, these violators will realize how important the city's libraries are to the community.

BRIAN PELTIER

Ludlow

---

night work in order to keep up with my other responsibilities. For example, I prepared the mailings at home. So, a certain dedication and feeling for the project was required.

For those of you facing such a problem or thinking about a program similar to ours, I have one recommendation: Don't ever let yourself get to the position where you need it. Our unacceptable backlog of overdues was an indirect result of budget cuts, but budget cuts do not make tasks go away and it is a false economy to ignore them. If you already have an extraordinary number of overdues or lost items and are thinking about pursuing them, by all means do it.

Do not let concerns about adverse publicity deter you. With a clear statement of your goals, which should stress fiscal responsibility and public service, and a well-planned media campaign, publicity will work in your favor.

FIGURE 1.6 Summary of Campaign Costs

Costs of Campaign

Henry's time	$6,000
Public Relation's time	$1,000
Miscellaneous time	$1,000
Postage (certified, return receipt, restricted delivery)	$900
Photocopying and supplies	$150
Total	**$9,050**

It's also important to understand that a program such as this would be impossible without the interest and full cooperation of the district attorney's office. I do not believe our results could be matched without the threat of legal action. In November 1996, we recovered fourteen more books, all on AIDS, that were due in 1992. The patron had been to court in August and was given a continuance that allowed him to avoid a criminal record if he returned the books within three months. The continuance was almost up, and without the legal threat I'm sure we never would have seen the books.

Patrons, too, respond positively to a library that is willing to pursue their library materials and maintain the services they support with their tax dollars. I think the public response is demonstrated by the elderly lady who came in and said to me, "Sir, you're the gentleman who's retrieving the library's materials, aren't you." I said, "Yes ma'am, we're trying." And she said, "Well I just wanted to thank you personally. You're doing a really great job." And as she was about to leave, she shook her finger and insisted, "If you ever need my help with those people, you just let me know and I'll come over and speak to them for you." For me, nothing summed up the benefits of the program better than that.

2 USE AN ELECTRONIC NOTIFICATION SYSTEM

by Judith C. Fuss

WILLIAMSBURG REGIONAL LIBRARY
WILLIAMSBURG, VIRGINIA

WHO WE ARE

Williamsburg, Virginia—synonymous with tradition and conservatism. How did this town's library find itself in 1994 passing up traditional paper for the high-tech world of electronic notification for its overdue and reserve items? The Williamsburg Regional Library is a small-to-medium-sized public library with 45,000 patrons and 900,000 yearly circulation, serving a suburban and rural population of more than 65,000. The service area extends over several counties and reaches from the densely populated industrial center of Newport News in the east to metropolitan Richmond in the west. The patron base includes more than 1,800 patrons residing outside the service area, one from as far away as Hawaii, and 3,300 students and faculty from the College of William and Mary. The library has been automated for over ten years, going online with Dynix, Inc., now Ameritech Library Services, in 1985–86.

THE WAY WE WERE

The often quiet town atmosphere of Williamsburg belies the active use that patrons make of library services. Reserves, always popular, jumped when patrons were provided the opportunity to place their own from public access terminals (PACs) in the library and from home via computer dial-in access. The library was looking at spiraling materials and postage costs for notices. By 1994, these costs had topped $10,000 per year and showed no sign of abating. The number of holds placed (and hold notices needing to be mailed) was growing significantly each month.

Patrons were notified of holds and overdue items by printed notice. To comply with state privacy statutes, notices were mailed in first-class envelopes. Three types of notices were printed: a Hold Notice, an Overdue Notice, and a Final Notice. Each patron for whom a hold had been activated the previous day received a Hold Notice. If the patron also had overdue items, a combined notice was printed. An Overdue Notice was generated for items twenty-eight days overdue. The number of overdue notices for each item had previously been pared from two notices to one in order to reduce costs. This meant that the first overdue contact was not made until the item had been out of the library for seven weeks. Final Notices were generated for items declared lost by the computer at ninety days. Eighty percent of notices printed were for reserve items. In addition to the cost of materials, significant staff time was consumed in printing and preparing as many as two hundred notices for the mail each day.

ENTER ENS

We purchased an electronic notification system (ENS) from Dynix, Inc., now Ameritech Library Services, as part of our automated library system and activated it on February 1, 1994. We made ENS our primary means of notification for holds and overdue materials. We continued to mail a final notice to notify patrons of replacement charges for materials that had been declared lost. With installation of ENS, the library anticipated a fifty percent reduction in staff time associated with reserves and overdues, as well as a ninety-five percent reduction in materials costs.

Patterns for hold and overdue calls made by ENS are customized for each library and set up in the ENS programming before installation. In Williamsburg, ENS calls patrons for holds on the day after each hold is activated and, if the item has not been picked up, again on day three. For those patrons called, no hold notices are generated. For patrons who are not called (see How ENS Works), a notice is automatically printed and mailed by the circulation staff. Using ENS has doubled the number of patron contacts for reserves.

ENS places calls for overdue items when they are seven, fourteen, and twenty-eight days overdue. Again, patrons who are called do not receive overdue notices. Notices are automatically printed for patrons who are not called. Using ENS has tripled the number of patron contacts for overdue materials. This increased contact has allowed us to shorten the span of time that materials are allowed to remain overdue in the system before being declared lost from ninety days to fifty-five days, thereby improving the chances of their return. A final notice is automatically printed if an item is overdue and still out at forty-five days, and the staff mails it just before the item is declared lost by the computer.

The library staff was looking forward to ENS and the work it would save them, but they realized that patrons might not all share their enthusiasm for this newest electronic member of the library family. Before activating ENS, we hung posters throughout the library building and distributed fliers to patrons announcing the new system. An article in the library newsletter explained how the system would work and the cost savings to be realized. Training sessions were conducted for staff on how ENS operates, changes in how patron information should be entered into the system to accommodate ENS, and dealing with patron inquiries about ENS calls.

HOW ENS WORKS

ENS runs on a stand-alone Wyse Decision 486 PC that is linked by direct connection to the main library computer. The basic operating parameters are set before shipment, in accordance with a pre-installation survey that the staff completes, but much of what the system does can be controlled locally. ENS places calls throughout the day over a dedicated modem line, following a script, that can be adjusted on site. Each library determines the text of one generic message for hold calls and one for overdue calls, although Ameritech does provide samples and suggestions. The messages are recorded on site; this provides a human rather than a synthesized voice. Many patrons see this as a plus, as some synthesized voices can be difficult to understand, especially for those with hearing impairments. Recording is done easily but requires a touch-tone modular telephone handset and a quiet location. Messages can be readily changed to meet patron needs or reflect changes in library procedures.

ENS starts daily operation at a time specified by each library. In Williamsburg, ENS begins her day at 10:00 A.M. By then the circulation staff has run morning reports and completed daily set-up duties and can be ready to answer any ENS-related questions that patrons may have. Prompted by the script, ENS automatically logs into the host system and, through a recall program, gathers information on patrons needing to be called that day for holds and overdues. This information is saved to a precall list, which is stored in the host system and also transmitted to the ENS PC. Information about patrons who cannot be called is compiled into a skipped calls report. ENS then disconnects from the host and continues working independently until it concludes its day of calling.

ENS places calls according to pre-set system parameters and information governing special circumstances that are provided in the phone code tables (see Setting Up Phone Information for ENS, p. 27). When a call is answered, either by a person or machine, ENS waits for three seconds of silence, then plays the appropriate prerecorded message. If the call is not answered, the number is cycled to the bottom of the calling list to call again later. The system loops through all calls on the precall list, then retries calls that were not successful earlier. Hold calls receive a higher priority than overdue calls in subsequent loops. Any unsuccessful calls remaining from the previous day are included in the precall list but receive a lower priority than first tries.

You can ensure that ENS does not call patrons during certain hours by programming breaks into the script. For example, if you do not wish calls to be placed over the dinner hour, you could program a break from 5:00 P.M. to 6:00 P.M. Eliminating break times will expand the available calling time if ENS is not able to complete all its daily calls on a regular basis. ENS will continue to loop through the precall list until all calls have been successfully completed, the preselected maximum number of loops has been reached, or the nightly shutdown time arrives. ENS then stops making calls, tabulates its daily activity, sends this information to the host system in the form of certain established reports, and "sleeps" until the next programmed wake-up time.

USING THE ENS MENU

Information about ENS can be obtained from the host system through the ENS menu, accessed from the circulation module. The various menu items provide tools to assist with patron inquiries, help track ENS functions, and customize the system's calling to suit local needs.

Figure 2.1 shows the circulation menu. To access the ENS menu (Figure 2.2), select menu item # 11, or enter MENS at the prompt.

FIGURE 2.1 Circulation System Menu

Williamsburg Regional Library
Circulation
MENU—CIRCULATION (MCIRC)

1.	CKO	ChecK Out
2.	CKI	ChecK In
3.	UPR	Update Patron Records
4.	IHU	In House Use
5.	GTS	Group TranSit
6.	CIV	Change Item Variables
7.	USI	Update Status of Items
8.	DEP	Day End Processing
9.	MHOLDS	Menu—HOLDS processing
10.	MOTHER	Menu—OTHER options
11.	MENS	Menu—Electronic Notification System

ENTER SELECTION:

FIGURE 2.2 ENS Menu

Williamsburg Regional Library
Circulation
MENU—ELECTRONIC NOTIFICATION SYSTEM (MENS)

1.	PHONE	PHONE call history
2.	RENSP	Report ENS Precalls
3.	RENSD	Report ENS Daily activity
4.	RENSU	Report ENS Daily unsuccessful calls
5.	RENSS	Report ENS Skipped phone numbers
6.	ENSPA	ENS Phone Analysis
7.	UENSE	Update ENS phone Exchanges

ENTER SELECTION:

PROBLEM-SOLVING USING PHONE CALL HISTORY

Since ENS operates on a stand-alone PC, its software is not fully integrated with the rest of the automated system. A record of phone calls made to patrons does not display in the patron record under the associated library item, as do blocks associated with printed notices. This information, however, is available using the ENS menu.

Selecting Phone Call History from the ENS menu brings up a prompt asking for a phone number. When a patron's phone number is entered, a screen such as that in Figure 2.3 appears. The phone number may be entered with or without separators.

FIGURE 2.3 Phone Call History

Phone : 2297577

Prefix... Date...........Name.........	Patron Id...	Msg..	Type	Suc
05–27–97 MOUSE, MICKEY	80873	HOLD	H	1
06–01–97 MOUSE, MICKEY	80873	PAST	P	1
06–22–97 MOUSE, MICKEY	80873	HOLD	H	1
06–30–97 MOUSE, MICKEY	80873	HOLD	H	0
07–10–97 MOUSE, MINNIE	80906	PAST	P	1
07–20–97 MOUSE, MICKEY	80873	HOLD	H	1
08–08–97 MOUSE, MINNIE	80906	HOLD	H	1
08–10–97 MOUSE, MICKEY	80873	HOLD	H	1
08–13–97 MOUSE, MICKEY	80873	HOLD	H	0
08–15–97 MOUSE, MICKEY	80873	HOLD	H	1

Enter phone # to search or 'Q' to quit :

The phone number is displayed at the top left of the screen. ENS calls to that number are listed below. The first column shows the date on which a call was placed. The second column lists the name of the patron called. If more than one patron in the system lists the same phone number, different names may be displayed in this column. The third column shows the ID number of the patron called. The fourth and fifth columns state the type of message left and the type of call placed, either hold (H) or pastdue (P). The last column indicates whether the call was successful or not. The number 1 means that a connection was made—a message was left with a person or a machine at the number called. Zero (0) means that no connection was made. The default period for this history is thirty days, but this can be extended through the report of daily activity in the ENS menu.

How might this information help you? The following situations are typical. Myrtle Fidget calls the reference desk. She is quite agitated. She received a call yesterday from "some horrible machine" saying that she has overdue library books. Why, she doesn't even have a library card. How can she, as she can't get out of the house to do anything for herself? What is the world coming to when machines can call innocent people on the telephone and accuse them of all sorts of terrible things. While Ms. Fidget is exhausting her complaints, the librarian accesses the phone call history from the ENS menu. She asks Ms. Fidget for her phone number so that she can check the library records and enters the number at the prompt. While Ms. Fidget rails against library inaccuracies, our stalwart librarian is studying the screen (Figure 2.4).

FIGURE 2.4 Detail from Phone Call History

Phone : 5556643

Prefix... Date....	Name...............	Patron ID...	Msg..	Type	Suc
05–27–95	SWOON, SALLY	80873	HOLD	H	1

She can see that ENS was attempting to contact Sally Swoon. A quick check of the patron index verifies that Ms. Fidget does not have a library card. Accessing Sally Swoon's record, using the patron ID listed in the phone call history, shows that her card was last updated twelve months ago. It is likely that her phone number has changed and needs correcting. Our librarian apologizes to Ms. Fidget for any disturbance ENS has caused and thanks her for helping to keep the library database current. Ms. Fidget apologizes for her tirade, explaining that two months ago she moved to a small apartment in Williamsburg after living thirty-two years in the same house in another state. The librarian describes the outreach services for homebound patrons and leaves Ms. Fidget eagerly awaiting a visit from the Bookmobile. Later a message can be added to Sally Swoon's record, asking for phone number verification to update her record. Adjustments can be made so that Ms. Fidget receives no more of Sally's library calls (see Report of Skipped Phone Calls).

General Brace calls for information about a hold book. He says that he was notified two days ago that a book was being held for him and he wants to know the title. A check of his record shows that no materials are currently being held. Using the phone call history and entering the phone number he gives brings up the name of another family member. ENS was contacting the general's daughter about a book held for her. So that ENS can remain affordable, its software is not designed to leave patron-specific messages. The message simply states that items reserved are now available. The general had assumed that this message was referring to him, when in fact it was directed to his daughter. The listing of specific patrons to whom calls are placed under the same phone number is found in the phone call history. Your library's policies concerning patron privacy will dictate how to proceed from this point.

USING THE PRECALL REPORT

Selecting item # 2 from the ENS menu (Figure 2.2) at any time after ENS has completed its wake-up procedures each day will bring up the precall report for that day. A sample precall report is shown in Figure 2.5. The first screen states the number of calls on the list and allows the option of printing or screening the list. This summary provides a snapshot of the ENS workload for the day and can alert you to unusual patterns that may indicate a problem.

FIGURE 2.5 Precall Report: Screen 1

Report contains 143 hold calls and 111 overdue calls

Output to:

Screen, press <Return>
Printer, press <P>
Auxiliary, press <A>
Quit, press <Q>

Make Selection ->

The report lists hold calls, then overdue calls, in alphabetical order by patron last name. The report date appears at the top of the page. The phone number, patron name, and patron identification number are listed for each call to be placed. This list is helpful if patrons have questions about a call they received that day.

For example, Martin Ames reports that he has just received a call that his hold book is in. He wishes more information as he does not remember placing any holds recently. A check of his record shows no items currently on hold for him. Verification of his phone number shows the correct listing in his record.

A check of the precall list for holds (Figure 2.6) shows that the phone number currently belonging to Martin Ames is also listed in the record of Merry Andrews.

FIGURE 2.6 Precall List for Holds

Precall Report for 08–31–95, 143 hold calls and 111 overdue calls

Phone........	Msg.	Name.............................	Patron Id
0000000	HOLD	ACK, MEL W	00
1111111	HOLD	ADAMS, JANE.	000
2222222	HOLD	AESOP, STORY.	00000
3333333	HOLD	ANDERS, AGATHA	0000
4444444	HOLD	ANDREWS, MERRY	00001
5555555	HOLD	BAILEY, SHAWN	001
6666666	HOLD	BARNS, RED.	00002

Using the patron ID listed to access her record, you see that Merry Andrews does have a book on hold. Since the addresses listed in the two records are different, it is likely that the phone listing for Merry needs updating. A message can be added to her record asking for phone number verification. Two options are available for assuring that Mr. Ames no longer receives calls for Merry: immediately clearing the phone field on Merry's record or, if you wish to retain the old number, placing an asterisk (*) in front of it (*444–4444). The asterisk tells ENS not to call this entry.

The precall report can also be used to gain specific patron information associated with generic calls. Mary Borne reports that she has just received a call about an overdue book and states that she does not have any books out at this time. She is sure there must be an error as she never allows books to become overdue. A check of her record confirms that she currently has no overdue items.

By checking the precall list for past-due calls (Figure 2.7), you can see that an overdue call was placed to the phone number listed in Mary Borne's record, but the call was directed to Enid Borne. Since the ENS message is generic, this information is not conveyed to the patron by ENS. Library policies regarding privacy and the release of patron information to individuals other than the patron will determine the course of action. ENS is operating correctly and the household has been alerted to overdue library materials.

FIGURE 2.7 Precall List for Past-Due Calls

Precall Report for 01–31–98, 143 hold calls and 111 overdue calls

Phone........	Msg.	Name...…	Patron ID
0000000	PAST	BORNE, ENID.	00000
1111111	PAST	COWARD, SHADE	00
2222222	PAST	DANE, ARLENE	0000
3333333	PAST	FORSYTE, GLINDA	00001
4444444	PAST	HOWARD, MERE	000
5555555	PAST	JOHNS, LESLEY	0000
6666666	PAST	JONES, JAMES	00002
8888888	PAST	RANSOME, WING	00003

DAILY ACTIVITY REPORT

At the end of each calling day, a report of ENS activity is compiled and sent to the host system. This information is then available through the ENS menu item Report of ENS Daily Activity. Reports are automatically saved for thirty days, but this time may be extended. When the report of daily activity ("3. RENSD" on Figure 2.2) is selected, a prompt appears: "Would you like a listing of available reports (y/n)?"

Answering *yes*, brings up a list of dates for which reports have been saved (Figure 2.8). If a particular date does not appear in the list, there is no report available for that date. This may reflect no activity scheduled, or it may indicate that ENS had a problem sometime during that day that kept it from sending a report to the host. At the bottom of the screen that lists report dates there is a prompt to change the number of days for which reports are saved.

FIGURE 2.8 Daily Activity Report

```
SORT ENS.CALLS        PAGE 1
ENS.CALLS.

08–01–97
08–02–97
08–03–97
08–04–97
08–05–97
```

Change the number of days to keep daily detail (y/n)

Entering a number greater than thirty at the change prompt increases the number of days for which reports are saved.

The daily activity report lists information in the same format as the precall report but for a specified date past. The report can be screened or printed. A number of patron complaints about hold calls not received on a particular day might prompt a look at the activity report for that date. If most or all of the calls are listed as unsuccessful, then there clearly was a problem with ENS on that day.

REPORT OF UNSUCCESSFUL CALLS

In addition to the complete list of calls made, the menu provides the option of selecting by date only those calls that were unsuccessful. Selecting the menu item for Report of ENS Daily Unsuccessful Calls and entering a date will bring up the screen with unsuccessful calls for that day (Figure 2.9).

FIGURE 2.9 Unsuccessful Calls Report

Unsuccessful Calls Report for 08–30–97, 10 records in report

Phone........	Msg.. Name.................	Patron Id...	Type	Suc
0000000	HOLD ACHESON, DEAN	20051	H	0
2111111	HOLD ALPS, SCOTT	74651	H	0
2222222	HOLD ANGLE, HORTENSE.	18564	H	0
3333333	HOLD AULD, GLADYS.	59564	H	0
5555555	HOLD BILLINGS, JOYCE.	74852	P	0
6666666	HOLD BORD, JARLENE	620	P	0
7777777	HOLD BUSCH, GEORGINE	68140	P	0
8888888	HOLD CHACHACA, CEILITO	67325	P	0
9999999	HOLD CHANG, PHYLLIS	68022	P	0

This report may be screened or sent to a printer. It might be used to print notices for mailing to these patrons.

REPORT OF SKIPPED PHONE CALLS

When preparing for ENS installation, each library is asked to select patron types or agencies that they do not wish ENS to call. Different patron types and agencies can be specified for each type of call. For example, you might want staff to be called about holds but not for overdues. You might want homebound patrons exempt from all calls. If the Bookmobile is set up as a separate agency and handles its own materials you might exclude those patrons from ENS calling. In addition, individual patron records can be marked for exclusion. Adding an asterisk (*) before a telephone number, or any entry in the phone field of a patron record, tells ENS not to call that entry. Any records marked with an asterisk on the precall list will not be called and will be listed in the Skipped Calls Report. If Sam Snurly complains bitterly about being called by a machine, adding an asterisk before the phone number in his patron record will assure that he is not called.

In Williamsburg, we used this feature to work around a problem we were having notifying students living on the College of William and Mary campus. The on-campus phone system provides voice mail for student numbers. However, accessing the voice mail requires intelligent interaction, beyond the scope of ENS. To access the voice mail of a particular student, numbers must be entered on a touch-tone phone. Unable to do this, but undaunted, ENS would wait for silence and then send forth a message into voice mail limbo. The call was recorded as successful, even though the student had no hope of receiving it. We entered an asterisk before all campus students' phone numbers. These were identified through a recall statement using a combination of patron type, address location, and phone exchange. This ensured that campus students would appear on the skipped calls report.

The first three columns of the skipped calls report list the patron's ID number, name, and phone number, or a notation entered in the phone field of the patron registration screen. The fourth column lists the type of notification required, and the last column gives the reason the call is being skipped. Most calls are on the report because an asterisk appears in the phone field or the patron type or agency has been excluded from calling. A "duplicate phone number" statement in this column indicates that another call of the same type was placed to the same number on that same day. No further action is needed. ENS is designed not to place multiple hold calls or overdue calls to a household on a given day so as not to annoy households with more than one active library patron.

Notices are automatically generated for patrons whose names appear on the skipped calls report except when the reason for the skipped call is a duplicate call of the same type being placed to the same number on the same day.

SETTING UP PHONE INFORMATION FOR ENS

ENS is a workhorse, busily dialing patrons hour after hour without ever taking a coffee break. But like all computers, it is precisely governed by specific parameters. It recognizes information only when entered in specific places in the system and in specific formats. It does not have the ability to interpret, interpolate, or look on the next line for information that is close to, but not exactly, what it is looking for. Like a library volunteer with blinders, ENS does precisely and literally what it is told to do, no more and no less. Before going online with ENS we reviewed our patron database, particularly in regard to phone entries, and adjusted certain areas. There are two built-in reports that help in doing this. They can also be used periodically to review the database once it is operational.

ENS PHONE ANALYSIS

The phone analysis provides a list of phone exchanges and area codes that are not represented in the phone codes table or that ENS does not understand and cannot dial. The first part of the report lists all patron records that contain phone-field entries that ENS cannot dial. This includes entries with an asterisk before the phone number, those with too many digits, and other nonconforming entries. Figure 2.10 is an example of the report showing the types of entries that might appear. Printed after the colon (:) is whatever has been entered in the phone field of the library record for the patron listed. This allows adjustments to be made to particular records.

FIGURE 2.10 Phone Analysis

REPORT OF UNIQUE EXCHANGE NUMBERS AND AREA CODES
(enclosed by parenthesis)

Unusual phone # for WILLINGHAM, JOHN D., ID# 00000 : DISCONNECTED
Unusual phone # for OKELLEY, BERNICE L., ID# 11111 : NONE
Unusual phone # for PIERCE, SAM., ID# 22222 : 764–4667 RM. 8129
Unusual phone # for DREW, NANCY , ID# 33333 : UNLISTED PHONE
Unusual phone # for CHAMP, KELLY M, ID# 44444 : NONE STAYING AT HOTEL TEMPORARILY
Unusual phone # for AGAR, RAUL C., ID# 55555 : 222–55776

Staff may want to keep notations, such as *Unlisted* or *Disconnected* to provide information as to why no phone number is entered in the record. Adding an asterisk will ensure that ENS does not try to call this number and that the patron's name will be listed on the skipped calls report. Phone numbers containing extensions or room numbers do not conform. These, too, will need the addition of an asterisk. Periodic use of this report assures that the database remains consistent. Following this is a list of all phone exchanges and area codes in the system. You can use this to identify local and long distance exchanges.

The last part of the report lists phone exchanges that do not appear in the phone codes table and the area codes in the system. This information is helpful in updating the table to reflect new exchanges that have been added to the patron database over time, invalid exchanges that have been entered inadvertently, or changes in area codes or dialing requirements.

PHONE CODES TABLE

The Phone Codes Table (Figure 2.11) is accessed through Update ENS Phone Exchanges on the ENS menu. The table provides special dialing instructions that override the system default instructions for the exchanges listed.

The telephone exchange is listed in the first column. Numbers that must be dialed before the exchange are listed in the next column. If your telephone system requires dialing 9 to connect with an outside line, this would be entered as a dialing prefix for all exchanges. A universal prefix such as this might also be set up as a system default thereby eliminating the need to enter it for each exchange in the table.

Before using the codes table, it is important to understand how ENS

FIGURE 2.11 Phone Codes Table

PHONE.CODES UPDATE PHONE NUMBER EXCHANGES			Total = 225	
EXCHANGE	DIALING PREFIX	DIALING SUFFIX		
1.	220			
2.	221			
3.	222	1,757		
4.	225	1,757		
5.	226	1,757		
6.	228	1,757		
7.	229			
8.	231	1,757		
9.	233	1,757		
10.	238	1,757		
11.	242	1,757		

#, New, Go #, Quit, Up :

handles phone numbers. ENS looks for numbers in spaces, reading left to right. If it finds seven numeric entries (555–2222), it recognizes this as a local call and dials the number as listed. If it counts ten numeric entries (000–555–1111), it recognizes this as a long distance call and automatically dials 1 and then the number listed. Using this information and considering the format in which phone entries are made to your patron records will determine what dialing prefixes will need to be entered in the codes table.

Our library staff enter patron phone numbers outside our area code (757) with the area code in the phone field of the patron record (e.g., 703–555–1111). When processing these phone numbers, ENS recognizes the ten numeric entries as a long-distance number and automatically prefixes a 1, as required, when dialing. All numbers within our area code are entered into the phone field of the patron record without the area code (e.g., 221–2222). When processing these phone numbers, ENS recognizes the seven numeric entries as a local number and does not add a prefix. I identified exchanges which are local calls. In 1994, these exchanges were all located within our area code and required no dialing prefix or adjustments through the phone codes table. Some exchanges within our area code are considered long distance calls and in 1994 required a 1, but not the area code, before dialing the phone number entered in the patron record. These exchanges were added to the codes table with "1" as the dialing prefix.

Since we first went online with ENS, the telephone company has made changes to dialing requirements, area codes, and local exchanges.

With adjustments to the phone codes table we have been able to accommodate these new requirements without data entry changes to patron records. Currently all long distance calls require the dialing of the area code, whether the call is placed inside or outside of that area code. Since phone exchanges within our area code are entered on patron records without the area code, we added 757 to the appropriate exchanges in the codes table where the prefix "1" had previously been entered. Whenever the telephone company alters which exchanges are considered local or long distance, I adjust the exchange listings in the code tables to reflect current dialing requirements. Recently an exchange outside our area code was designated as local. Since phone numbers with this exchange have been entered in patron records with the area code, ENS, using system-default parameters, would recognize these as long distance numbers, which they no longer are. Entries in the codes table, however, override system defaults. By entering the new local exchange in the codes table without a dialing prefix or area code, ENS will dial these phone numbers as entered in the patron record (e.g., 804–333–4567, without the prefix 1) matching new telephone company requirements. Time consuming reentry of data in patron records is avoided.

WAS IT WORTH IT?

Even during the first month of operation, when holds placed before activation of ENS were still generating notices, the library saw a 50 percent reduction in staff time and a 75 percent reduction in materials costs associated with notices. Real savings for the first year, based on usage of supplies, amounted to almost $9,000, meaning that ENS more than paid for itself in that time. Patrons receive faster notification of reserves, and items turn over more quickly on the hold shelves than before ENS. The library has been able to reduce the number of days items are held on the reserve shelves by two days. Despite our initial fears, patrons' responses to ENS have been overwhelmingly positive. They appreciate the faster notification. Some show up at the circulation desk to pick up reserves minutes after being called. During the initial transition, when some holds were still generating notices, many patrons expressed disappointment if they received a notice instead of being called by our computer. They wanted to be contacted by our new "gadget." Only a handful of patrons continue to request that they not be called by machine. Although ENS initially required significant time for setup and adjustment, after the first year only minimal monitoring is needed to keep things running smoothly. Was the journey worth the trip? Definitely.

3 USE A CREDIT BUREAU
by Melody Moxley and Jeff Hall

ROWAN PUBLIC LIBRARY
SALISBURY, NORTH CAROLINA

The Rowan Public Library (RPL) system serves a county of 110,605 in Piedmont, North Carolina, with a headquarters, two branches, an Adult Outreach service, and a "Stories to Go" service that provides programs and circulating materials to area child-care centers. The library's budget for FY 1995–96 was $1,650,542, with an annual circulation in excess of 500,000 items per year.

Director Phillip Barton and his staff have demonstrated a serious commitment to accurate and timely handling of overdue materials and library users who do not return materials on time. Since June 1992 RPL has integrated use of the Credit Bureau of Rowan County into its overdue policies and procedures, and this has proven an effective means of retrieving library materials.

Use of a credit bureau is the result of a lengthy process of evaluation of overdue policies and procedures. Prior to 1980, RPL sent four notices to users who had overdue materials: three overdue notices and one bill. All record keeping of fines, overdues, and reserves was handled manually by the circulation staff. As circulation grew, this manual system occupied more and more staff time. By 1980, the library administration realized that it was impossible to maintain this system with existing staff resources.

The administration reviewed and revised overdue procedures with three goals in mind: 1) to streamline overdue procedures; 2) to maintain accurate circulation records; and 3) to hold users accountable for unreturned materials. The four-notice system was replaced by a six-day grace period during which users would not be charged fines for overdue materials followed by the mailing of two notices: an overdue notice at two weeks and a bill at four weeks. The six-day grace period enabled the circulation staff to maintain other circulation functions without sacrificing accuracy of records or user responsibility.

In time, however, the administration realized that current overdue procedures—sending notices, keeping charges on users' records, and even denying borrowing privileges to delinquent users—were not sufficient to provide adequate guardianship of materials purchased with public funds. As many libraries have discovered, delinquent users often find other ways to borrow materials, such as using the card of a friend or family member. Users will also decide to forego their borrowing privileges in order to retain materials or avoid paying replacement costs.

After discussing and investigating several alternative methods of collection, RPL's administration decided that delinquent users who owed $50.00 or more in replacement costs would be taken to the Small

Claims Court of Rowan County. The circulation librarian filed the appropriate documents with the court. All cases taken to court were decided in the library's favor. The library's actions garnered no unfavorable publicity; moreover, the response we received from the public indicated that the library's stance was viewed as reasonable given the provocation.

This system for pursuing delinquent library users, which was put into place in 1980, had the effect of lowering the library's overdue rate. In 1983, while the overdue rate at the last due date was 13.5 percent, by eight weeks past the due date the rate fell to 0.35 percent. At one year, the overdue rate was 0.44 percent. This reduction in rate is attributable to a system of accurate record-keeping followed by such efforts at collections as were possible given available information and staff time. This 0.44 percent rate at one year was significantly lower than the 1.15 percent mean for libraries reported in the 1983 survey conducted by Robert Burgin and Patsy Hansel.

Although the small claims procedure was effective, it could only be used in a small number of cases, because the manual overdue system made it difficult to determine the total value of items held overdue by a delinquent patron. Also, in many cases the library staff could not take a delinquent borrower to court because they could not locate a valid address, which was needed by the Sheriff's Office in order to serve a summons. Many delinquent users had simply moved away taking library materials with them. The library's only recourse was to list these delinquent and nonlocatable users with the Credit Bureau of Rowan County, an action that netted negligible results during the mid- to late 1980s. And regardless of the result, the staff time devoted to preparing documents and appearing in small-claims court was considerable. On average it took two hours per delinquent user to prepare court documents. Subsequently, a staff member might sit in court as many as five hours waiting for a single case to be called.

During the mid-1980s, the circulation staff continued to maintain accurate records and to retrieve overdue materials by denying borrowing privileges to delinquent users. At that time, however, the entire library staff became involved in a building-needs study, which precluded pursuing delinquent users through small-claims court. In 1986, the board of trustees of Rowan Public Library proposed, and the Rowan County board of commissioners approved, for public referendum a $2.5 million bond to expand the headquarters library. In November 1986 the bond passed, and the design and construction of a new library ensued. As part of the building program, the library evaluated automated library systems, and it became impossible to devote the time needed to pursue delinquent users through small-claims court. Consequently, fewer cases were listed with the local credit bureau.

In 1989, the library selected an automated library system developed by NSC, Inc. Circulation functions were fully automated by November 1989.

No statistics are available to determine overdue rates for the early 1990s, but the more accurate record-keeping and the lowering of human error made possible through automation did seem to lower the percentage of materials overdue at any given time. In addition, users perceived an automated system as more accurate than the previous manual system, and so were less apt to challenge overdue notices.

Despite the greater accuracy and more timely processing of returned materials with an automated system, Rowan Public Library has, as all libraries do, continued to have users who fail to return materials. We are still committed to responsible guardianship of materials purchased with public money, realizing that every unreturned item is an item that is unavailable to other citizens who contributed towards its purchase.

In 1992 Jeff Hall, circulation services supervisor, investigated credit reporting and collections services options available to the library through the Credit Bureau of Rowan County. The library administration recommended to the board of trustees that any adult user with any item more than eighteen weeks overdue, regardless of replacement cost, be listed with the credit bureau. The board of trustees approved this suggested policy in June 1992 (see Appendix A). Hall immediately began to oversee the compilation of delinquent user records. He also collaborated with the credit bureau staff in the development of procedures for reporting these individuals to the bureau on a regular basis. The first report was issued in July 1992.

Since its inception, use of the credit bureau has proven an effective method of retrieving overdue library materials. Its effectiveness lies in the fact that in order for the delinquent library user to obtain almost any kind of loan the library account must first be cleared. So notified, delinquent users have returned materials, paid for their overdues, and paid fines so that they can qualify for home mortgages, car loans, personal loans, and, in some cases, apartment rentals. Another point of effectiveness lies in the fact even though a library user may move, the credit history follows.

What follows is a description of how the Rowan Public Library presently handles materials that library users do not return, from the first overdue notice to the final report to the credit bureau.

Once library materials are overdue the automated circulation system generates a check-out block. Three overdue notices are sent to the user: one at two weeks past the due date, one at four weeks, and one at six weeks. These notices merely inform the library user of specific overdue materials and request prompt return. The notices are generated by the library's automated circulation system (see Appendix B).

At sixteen weeks overdue, a billing notice is sent to the user. This notice informs the user that the materials must be returned and fines paid within two weeks or the account will be turned over to the Credit Bureau of Rowan County. These notices are also generated automatically by the library's circulation system.

At eighteen weeks past due, the library shelves are checked to make sure the materials have not been shelved by mistake. If the materials are neither located on the shelves by the library staff nor returned by the user before eighteen weeks past due, the user's account is recorded on a trade line maintenance form and sent to the Credit Bureau of Rowan County. The circulation staff changes the status of the long overdue materials checked out by adults to C (credit bureau), which shows as "Credit Bureau" in the online catalog. Although it is possible to list the accounts of juveniles on a parent's credit record, Rowan Public Library does not exercise this capability because of the extensive labor required to determine the identity of the responsible adult.

When the credit bureau performs trade line maintenance on the user's credit file the account is listed as overdue and unpaid. This listing stays on the user's credit history for seven years.

If any item is returned by a user listed with the credit bureau, a message appears on the circulation terminal screen informing staff that the item has been listed with the credit bureau. The staff member reports the return of the materials to the circulation associate, who then sends a letter to the credit bureau requesting that the trade line maintenance listing be removed.

Public libraries should be aware that many credit bureaus will refuse to remove a trade maintenance listing. They often will mark the record as paid but late, which may result in a previously delinquent library user (who has since cleared the account with the library) being unable to obtain credit, loans, or rental housing.

While the Credit Bureau of Rowan County will remove trade line maintenance listings when the library informs them that an account has been cleared, they do so reluctantly. Barbara Beck, supervisor of trade line maintenance with the Credit Bureau of Rowan County, recommends that listings not be removed unless they are recorded by mistake. She contends that by removing a listing that has been paid, an inaccurate credit record is created.[1]

The RPL administration has decided to ask the credit bureau to remove the listing once the account is cleared, as it appears unfair to penalize an individual after they have paid for or returned materials and paid all fines.

Once a month, the circulation associate reviews all adult overdue accounts still outstanding after six months. Accounts representing a value of more than one hundred dollars worth of library materials are removed from trade line maintenance and turned over to the collection division of the credit bureau. The amount of one hundred dollars as a minimum for collection activity is set by library policy; the credit bureau will pursue collection activities on accounts as small as twenty-five dollars.

The materials listed on the user's accounts are then withdrawn from the library catalog. A "Collections" block is manually entered, replacing the automatic check-out block, to continue blocking any future check outs by the delinquent library user.

At this point, all payments must be made to the collections division of the credit bureau; the library will no longer accept the materials for return or payment of replacement cost and associated fines. Delinquent users who come to the library to return or pay for items that have been listed with the collections division are told by library staff that they must pay at the credit bureau. The collections division takes a portion of the payment as its fee: for accounts less than one year old the fee is 33 percent; for accounts one year old or older the fee is 50 percent.

Once the library notifies the collection division of a delinquent account, the division issues two notices to the delinquent library user. The division then makes several telephone calls during a thirty-day period to encourage the delinquent library user to pay off the account. At the end of thirty days, the collection activity is reported as public record on the credit file and remains there for seven years.

During an eight-month period—April 1995 through November 1995—Rowan Public Library listed 455 delinquent users with the Credit Bureau of Rowan County to perform trade line maintenance. During this period, 217 library users listed for trade line maintenance cleared their accounts by returning or paying for overdue materials. Collection activities were less successful. Of 106 accounts turned over for collection, only two have been paid.

The combination of library automation and the consistent use of the credit bureau to list overdue accounts has resulted in lower overdue rates. In July of 1995 the overdue rate for library materials two weeks overdue was 1.6 percent. The overdue rate for materials one year overdue was 0.33 percent as compared to 0.44 percent in 1983.

Public reaction to the use of the credit bureau has been largely positive. Many library users have commented that they believe it is good that the library actively pursues delinquent borrowers in this manner. Also, by indicating in the library's online catalog that an item is currently overdue and is listed on the credit record of a delinquent patron, a subtle warning about refusing to return overdue library materials is issued. Naturally, as a matter of confidentiality the names of the delinquent library users do not appear on the catalog.

Use of a credit bureau as part of a library's overdue policy has requirements.

First, it is imperative that the library possess an accurate means of tracking overdue library materials. Next, the library must join a local credit bureau or hire a collection agency. The library should obtain approval from its governing board or officials before it undertakes such a serious course of action. The governing body or officials need to understand that using a collection agency or credit bureau may adversely affect an individual's credit history, perhaps permanently. It may also prevent the library from seeking a legal remedy such as prosecution or civil actions.

A further issue arises when the library must decide if it wants to pursue juvenile delinquent accounts. It is possible to list these accounts on the parents' credit record if the library requires a parent to cosign their child's registration card, thereby accepting responsibility for the child's account.

And finally, while using a credit bureau can be an effective method, a library that employs it must be diligent in reporting payments on accounts to the credit listing or collection agency. Otherwise, library users who have cleared their accounts may suffer needlessly.

The Rowan Public Library administration has a history of taking overdues seriously to act as responsible guardians of materials purchased with public money. Our commitment to this role has never wavered, although our approaches to performing it successfully have. While our procedures and policies are always open to improvement and may evolve further, we feel that our overdue rate, which is much lower than the current national average, reflects the effectiveness of our overdue policy and procedures.

REFERENCES

1. Barbara Beck, telephone conversation with author, 13 December 1995.

APPENDIX A: OVERDUES AND FINES POLICY

Adopted June 24, 1992 by the Board of Trustees of Rowan Public Library

SERVICE OBJECTIVE

Rowan Public Library aims to develop and maintain a materials collection which is responsive to the needs and interests of the local community and to provide ready access to those materials. An important part of maintaining the collection and access to it includes retrieving overdue materials so they are available for the public to use. The library will aim to do this in a manner that is both fair and effective.

FINES

The library charges fines for overdue materials as an incentive for people to return the materials on time. Fines are charged on all materials and equipment, except children's materials labeled "E." The fine shall commence the day after the material is due and will continue accumulating until the material is returned, or until the fine reaches the maximum accumulation. Fines may be waived at the discretion of the supervising librarian.

SCHEDULE OF FINES

MATERIAL	FINE	MAXIMUM FINE ACCUMULATION
Books (except "E" books)	$.10/day	$4.00
Audiovisual materials (except "E" materials)	$.10/day	$4.00
Videos	$.10/day	$20.00
Interlibrary loans	$1.00/day	$20.00
Unclaimed interlibrary loans	$4.00/item	
Equipment	$1.00/day	$100.00

APPENDIX B: NOTIFICATION OF OVERDUES

An attempt will be made to notify a library user of overdue materials according to the following schedule:

First notice—two weeks or more overdue
Second notice—four weeks or more overdue
Third notice—six weeks or more overdue
Fourth notice—sixteen weeks or more overdue; bill and letter informing user that the past due account will be submitted to the Credit Bureau for further action will be sent to all adult users

SUSPENSION OF BORROWING PRIVILEGES

A library user's borrowing privileges will be suspended if any of the following conditions exist:

1. The user has any library materials two weeks or more overdue.
2. The user owes $4.00 or more in library fees or fines.
3. The user exceeds two claims returned.

A library user's borrowing privileges will be reinstated if the condition causing suspension is resolved.

USE OF THE CREDIT BUREAU

The library will use the local credit bureau in handling adult accounts sixteen weeks or more overdue.

1. Accounts which total $100.00 or less will be listed on the user's credit record as an unpaid account.
2. Accounts which exceed $100.00 will be listed on the user's credit record as an unpaid account and the Credit Bureau Collection Service will be instructed to collect the cost of materials and associated fines.

USE OF LITIGATION

The library may use litigation in pursuing unusually large overdue accounts. Such action will be recommended by staff and decided on a case by case basis by the Board of Trustees.

DEFINITION OF ADULT LIBRARY USER

For the purposes of this policy an adult library user is defined as anyone at least 18 years of age.

4 USE A COLLECTION AGENCY

By Susan Swanton

GATES PUBLIC LIBRARY
ROCHESTER, NEW YORK

At the Gates Public Library we have used a collection agency to recover overdue items and accounts for twelve years. Ours is an active suburban library on the west side of Rochester, N.Y., with a materials budget of $140,000 and an annual circulation approaching half a million. We serve a town of close to 30,000 nighttime population and an even larger daytime population. We have strong media and nonfiction collections and extensive audiovisual services. Because we are so close to the city of Rochester, our overdues statistics more clearly resemble those of urban libraries than those of smaller libraries.

Before we decided to try a collection agency, we had already used the usual sources for dealing with overdues: we sent invoices for replacement after our first and second overdue notices had been ignored, and at the circulation desk we kept a list of serious delinquents whose privileges were blocked. We did everything manually since we were not yet online. We had also used a small claims process through the town courts, which was much too time consuming for the number of seriously delinquent cases in our library. At another point we tried using town volunteers from the auxiliary police to collect overdue items from patrons' homes. However, they were frustrated both with the number of times they had to return to a home and with the low recovery rate.

Then, in 1983, Dan Keane of Albert Damian Associates, Syracuse, N.Y., gave a talk to our local chamber of commerce. After hearing his many tips about recovery of past due bills, I decided this could benefit our busy suburban library. Also, using a third party relieved library staff of entanglements in the often involved and difficult family circumstances surrounding delinquent patrons. This particular collection agency showed great willingness to work with us, and their expertise with this difficult area of managing losses was evident. We have talked to other collection agencies, but so far none has ever offered us a deal that is as good and hassle-free as what we have with our current agency.

The library board was impressed with the possibilities and on March 14, 1984, voted unanimously to designate Albert Damian Associates as Gates Public Library's official collection agency. The library board continues to review our collection agency policy and to refine it. The latest version was adopted on November 13, 1991 (Figure 4.1).

To be sure that patrons are aware of the consequences of serious overdues, we refer to our use of a collection agency in our card appli-

---

FIGURE 4.1

Gates Public Library Collection Agency Procedure, Rev.

POLICIES:

1. All outstanding overdue accounts of $25 or more in material and fines, 30 days after a BFR or tracer letter is sent, will be turned over. Patrons owing *fines only* will not be turned over.
2. Once turned over, patrons are asked to phone Damian for instructions on payment and clearing their account.
3. Once turned over, we do not accept their material or items back (unless Director agrees to a settlement).
4. When turned over, patron is stopped in the database. On receipt of their payment from Damian, their record is cleared in the database.
5. Damian receives one-third of the turnover price. Gates Public Library receives two-thirds.
6. When turning over minors, their parents/guardians are listed as the responsible adult.
7. The collection agency can not collect from anyone who has declared bankruptcy.

PROCEDURES:

1. *Regular turnovers*—Accounts $25 or more, not responding to BFR or tracer letter, after 30 days are turned over to Damian.
   a. All BFR letters have envelopes stamped with "forwarding and address correction requested" to be sure it arrives properly or it is returned to library. If returned, the envelope with notation from the post office is stapled to our copy of the BFR letter. The patron is then considered a "skip". Skips are also turned over. Keeping the returned envelope shows patron that we did in fact attempt to send the correct amount of notices and the post office considered them undeliverable.
   b. Once turnover list is assembled, all items are again checked against patron's record to be sure it is still attached.
   c. If still listed as overdue, then all items are checked against the shelves.
   d. If not on shelf, then Damian forms are filled out (with replacement prices listed and 25% service fee added); prices changed in database to cover service fee; copy specific holds placed on each item and collection agency message placed in notefield.
   e. Completed Damian forms are sent to their Syracuse office and entered into their computer.

2. *Settlement in Full*—Damian doesn't encourage our handling of Settlements, but will accept them.
   a. The material must be personally inspected by the Director for condition.
   b. Patron must write two checks to pay the account in full.
      1. One check payable to Gates Public Library for the maximum overdue fine plus the processing fee.
      2. One check payable to Albert Damian Associates for one-third of the turnover price.
   c. Books get reinstated into the collection.

FIGURE 4.1 (cont.)

3. *Improper Return*—If turned over items are found at the desk or in the bookdrop, when discharged the collection agency hold appears. Item is then reattached to patron record, hold reapplied and Improper Return letter sent to both patron and Damian (Syracuse). The letter states items were returned and since they were turn overs: patron has 30 days to pick them up before they are considered a donation and their account is still active with Damian. After items remain here for approximately 60 days, we delete the barcode numbers from the database, and may choose to give them new barcode numbers and reinstate them into the collection.

4. *Close outs*—Usually after a year, when Damian has used up all their means of collecting from a patron, they consider them a close out and delete them from their database. They periodically send us a list of close outs. We still keep the Damian notation on their record and they are still not able to check out material.

    a. At the time of close out, all accounts turned over prior to Nov. 13, 1991, will have their item prices recalculated back down to 125%.

        Prime Reasons For Close Outs:

        1. Skip—cannot locate
        2. Exhausted all collection efforts: consider uncollectible.
        3. Debtor refuses to pay amicably: suit not advised at this time.

COURT CASES:

1. We occasionally receive information from Damian notifying us they are ready to seek legal action against particular patron.
2. We would have to advance a collection fee, previously $55 but now we are told, considerably higher.
3. The Director makes the decision whether or not to take legal action. It is based on information that Damian gives us as to the pursuability of the case and whether or not it is worth the money for the town to issue a manual check which later gets reported to the Board as an "in lieu of claim."

    An example: We recently were asked to advance money for legal action against a patron who worked in a local bar. His account was for under $100. The Director didn't regard the employer as stable and felt the patron could easily leave his job at the bar to avoid having his wages put in jeopardy. We did not pursue.

4. If court case not pursued, we return the legal paperwork to Damian and their regular account remains on file.
5. It has been our practice not to take on a court case for less than $250, although legally, we may.

Policy Approved 2/2/91;
revised 11/13/91

cation forms for both adults and minors (Figures 4.2 and 4.3), and we include the following words in our fines and fees schedule:

COLLECTION AGENCY
Delinquent accounts may be turned over to the library's collection agency, and the agency fee added to the balance due.

Damian Associates have helped us handle our overdues problem by urging us to bill delinquent patrons in a timely manner. If the materials are not returned, we turn over the accounts to the collection agency 90 to 120 days after the due date.

Damian Associates start by sending the delinquent patrons two letters, and if the accounts are not settled after two letters, they start to make phone calls. We receive a Debtor's Status Report from Damian Associates, which lists all of our outstanding accounts, a statement on accounts paid partly or in full, and our part of any funds recovered.

We know when Damian Associates are at work because we begin to get phone calls from apologetic delinquent patrons who are desper-

---

FIGURE 4.2   Application for Library Card

GATES PUBLIC LIBRARY APPLICATION FOR LIBRARY CARD   Date:_____

Name: _____
                          Last   First   Middle
Local Address

Street: _____ Town: _____

City: _____ State: _____ Zip Code: _____ Phone: _____

Permanent Address (if different from above)

Street: _____

City: _____ State: _____ Zip Code: _____ Phone: _____

I agree to assume responsibility for all materials borrowed on this card and to abide by the rules of the Monroe County Library System and the Gates Public Library. I understand that I must report the loss or theft of my card immediately and that I am responsible for any use made of a lost or stolen card prior to my report, including liability for any charges incurred. I am aware that Gates Public Library reserves the right to refer delinquent accounts to a collection agency.

Signature: _____

ID USED:_____ STAFF: _____

Form 81

FIGURE 4.3 Application for Children's Library Card

GATES PUBLIC LIBRARY APPLICATION FOR CHILDREN'S LIBRARY CARD   Date: _____

Child's Name: _____
                          Last   First   Middle

Grade: _____ Age: _____

To be completed by PARENT or LEGAL GUARDIAN: My child has my permission to have a library card. I understand that children's and adult collections, which includes full Internet resources, are accessible to children and I accept responsibility for all selection of materials and any loss incurred through my child's use of the library. I understand that I must report the loss or theft of my child's card immediately and that I am responsible for any use made of a lost or stolen card prior to my report, including liability for any charges incurred. I am aware that Gates Public Library reserves the right to refer delinquent accounts to a collection agency.

Adult's Name: _____

Address: _____ Town: _____

City: _____ State: _____ Zip Code: _____ Phone: _____

Signature: _____

ID USED: _____   STAFF: Form 81a

---

ate to cut a deal. Under extenuating circumstances we may accept a settlement in full, but both the library staff and Damian Associates prefer to have the debtors deal with them. It is much smoother and much easier. Because our library does not have any check-writing privileges, to handle a settlement in full we have to ask the customer to bring in two checks (one for the library fines and one for the agency fees) plus all the overdue materials. Often materials that have been out of the collection for an extended period of time and stored in less than desirable circumstances are in no condition to return to the collection. Furthermore, it is too time consuming to handle these transactions at a busy circulation desk.

It is important to note that in working with a collection agency, we do not get the materials back unless we agree to accept a settlement in full from the patron. It is always the local library's option to decide whether to accept settlements in full. We decided that we preferred to let the collection agency collect the replacement costs. After all, the delinquent customer had the opportunity to respond to each of our notices and bills *before* we sent the account to our collection agency. If materials have been out of the collection for some time or perhaps stored under less than ideal circumstances, it may be preferable to receive the replacement costs rather than the materials. Also, collection agency money is revenue in our budget.

It is amazing how many delinquent patrons, after they have paid their accounts, return to use the library. And when they return they don't let their overdue accounts get seriously overdue! Oddly enough, I think there is some element of "saving face" in dealing with a collection agency rather than with the neighborhood public library.

As for the library, there is security in knowing that the collection agency personnel know the law and are effective in recovery—otherwise they don't stay in business. Our collection agency has given us some helpful advice in understanding delinquent patrons and knowing how to respond to them. Here are some tips from Dan Keane of Albert Damian Associates.

1) A public library is similar to a hospital emergency room. Both extend credit without a credit check. (Both hospital emergency rooms and public libraries experience a 20 percent collection rate return.)

2) Consider whether your library will allow parents with delinquent materials to sign for and use their minor children's cards. It may be a poor risk because adults who are not responsible for their own debts are not likely to honor their children's debts. (In our library, the parent who signs permission for a minor child to use the library is the one referred to the collection agency, even though the child has full borrowing privileges.) Note: you cannot refer a minor, unless legally emancipated, to a collection agency.

3) Even if you decide not to refer patrons with fines only to your collection agency, one way to help with the recovery of these unpaid fines is to send a form letter thanking them for returning their materials, but adding, "however, you still have fines due which will prohibit your use of the library." (Gates does this.)

4) In letters, use no more than three sentences in each paragraph. Limit sentences to twenty-three words. Use words with three syllables or fewer. Target letters at fifth-grade reading level.

5) For people who claim they never received library notices say, "We monitor everything going out in the mail and stamp our bills forwarding and address correction requested. Could it be you are having a problem with your mail delivery?" This lets patrons know you are not buying the story, but at the same time it gives them an out and allows you to continue dealing with the overdue problem at hand.

6) Remember, library bills are considered low priority in people's bill paying schedule. Mortgages, car payments, and credit cards must be paid before people worry about their library bills.

We have been very satisfied with Albert Damian's success in col-

		Value of				Recovery Rate (Percent of	Recovery of
Period	No. of Accounts	Accounts Placed	Payments To date	Commissions To date	PIF*	Accounts Placed)	Library Revenues
1984	58	$7,270	$1,732	$796	15	26.7	not itemized
1985	123	$10,746	$3,225	$1,513	31	30.3	in budget
1986	14	$1,291	$546	$240	6	42.3	$913.77
1987	79	$8,026	$2,026	$950	19	26.0	$672.43
1988	102	$10,352	$1,855	$905	22	18.9	$890.87
1989	66	$6,347	$1,447	$884	13	27.3	$755.58
1990	106	$10,592	$2,300	$1,125	31	26.0	$736.67
1991	79	$8,719	$1,505	$647	23	28.7	$859.64
1992	31	$1,566	$109	$36	7	7.0	$960.99
1993	92	$6,069	$1,666	$552	23	32.8	$948.32
1994	21	$1,488	$443	$147	7	41.6	$628.47
1995	9	$1,276	$151	$50	1	11.8	$69.00
1996	13	$1,039	$90	$30	2	8.7	$62.86
Total	819	$77,109	$19,090	$8,601	209	27.2	$7,498.60

FIGURE 4.4 Overdues payments collected by agency 1984–1996

*PIF is the number of delinquent accounts paid in full. Many of these may be partial payments at any given point during the year.

lecting fines and replacement costs (Figure 4.4). While the average recovery rate for public libraries is 20 percent, we had a 27.2 percent recover rate from the time period March 1984 to November 1996. Although these were accounts paid in full, the revenues recovered only 10 percent of the value of the materials lost. Still, it is revenue.

At the Gates Public Library, we liked our "contingency" fee arrangement with Albert Damian Associates, which meant no financial outlay for our library. The delinquent customer who finally pays Damian Associates provides the agency's cut (33 percent) of the total recovered. So our relationship with Albert Damian Associates is a win-win situation:

1. There is no financial outlay or retainer for the library to pay.
2. The library can consult with them and benefit from their experience.
3. They take over after library statements have been ignored.
4. They know the federal and state collection statutes.
5. They know the most effective way to collect the essentially uncollectible.
6. Patrons know the library takes the return of overdue library materials seriously because we tell them when they apply for a card that we use a collection agency.
7. Some delinquent patrons seem to respond better to a collection agency because it is a third party.
8. Politically it looks good to retrieve whatever funds we can.

In 1988, the county library system, of which we are a member, selected GEAC as our automation vendor. With a centralized patron database and automated alerts, our recovery of overdues (before referral to the agency) improved, but our collection agency revenue continued to average between $860 and $900 a year. In 1993, the county library system migrated to CARL, and we did not have usable reports for our collection agency until fall 1995, when CARL began to produce them. Because we did not have these reports, our use appears to have declined in 1994–95, but the system now produces reports of accounts over $25 that are seriously delinquent (90 days or more), and we have been able to catch up with the backlog of delinquencies.

As of December 1997, we had 361 active accounts going back six years for a total of $31,520.12. The average account total is $87.31. Of the 361 accounts, about seven are "skips" (no known address) whom Damian Associates is trying to locate for us.

Being part of an automated county system is a factor in our fines and overdue materials. The libraries in the county all have different circulation policies, and sometimes we discover that we have lost materials to a minor registered as an adult at another library. Sometimes other area libraries lose materials to our delinquent patrons. A note on the patron's record and on the overdue materials helps to alert the other libraries. Enough of the area libraries use collection agencies so there is good support among our fellow libraries.

Forty percent of our users are not town residents, and seriously overdue patrons who are referred to our collection agency average 60 percent nonresidents. At least half of the remaining 40 percent, the Gates residents, are apartment dwellers and, judging by the returned mail, have minimal roots in the community. Hence one can easily conclude that the vast majority of accounts that will be referred to a collection agency will *not* be local home owners. At least that has been the case with our library.

We have had some interesting experiences with collection agency referrals. Although most of the delinquent cases are handled without library involvement, twice the library has been listed as a creditor in bankruptcy hearings, and once I even went to court to represent the library. We have learned that you cannot pursue someone who has declared bankruptcy, not even someone who forgot to list you as a creditor; nor can you pursue anyone on welfare. In the past you could not pursue anyone on active military service although apparently that has changed.

Once we referred an account of over $600, only to find out that the delinquent patron involved was a minor registered as an adult at another library. We had no idea that he was a minor or that he had lost his library card and never reported it missing. We had to withdraw that account.

We have also had hard luck stories, family squabbles, and our share of "lost while moving" vignettes. This is not particularly surprising, since by the time an account has been referred to a collection agency there's generally some problem behind the lack of responsiveness.

Based on the success we have had at Gates, I would certainly encourage other libraries to seriously consider following our example. Look at your pattern of loss, and contact a local collection agency. In addition, consider contacting the American Collectors Association, Inc., 4040 West 70th Street 55435, P.O. Box 39106, Minneapolis, MN 55429–0106; Telephone (612) 926–6547; fax (612) 926–1624. See appendixes a, b, and c for American Collectors Association information.

I only wish we had discovered the benefits of using a collection agency a decade before we did. Using Albert Damian Associates has made it possible for the library to retrieve delinquent fines at a rate above the national average for libraries, has helped many of our patrons to be more responsible borrowers, and has freed the staff to provide better service to library users.

Anyone who wants further information about the Gates Public Library and our successful use of a collection agency in dealing with overdue materials and unpaid fines can contact me: Susan Swanton, Library Director, Gates Public Library, 1605 Buffalo Road, Rochester, NY 14624; phone: (716) 247–6446; email:sswanton@mcls. rochester.lib.ny.us/

APPENDIX A: FACTS ABOUT THE COLLECTION SERVICE INDUSTRY

American Collectors Association, Inc.

THE SCOPE OF THE INDUSTRY

- According to the 1995 Top Collection Markets Survey, in 1994 an estimated 290.3 million accounts, totaling $84.2 billion, were placed for collection with professional third-party collection businesses.
- According to ACA's 1994 Collection Index Survey, the estimated average national recovery rate for 1994 was 18.41 percent.
- Professional, third-party collection agencies collected and returned more than $15.5 billion to the U.S. economy.
- The average age of past due accounts referred to professional debt collection businesses is about eight months.
- Between one-third and one-half of the accounts that are referred for collection require the collection service to find information about how to locate the people involved.
- The federal law regulating third-party collection businesses is the Fair Debt Collection Practices Act, passed in 1977. The Federal Trade Commission enforces the federal law. Thirty-three states have either licensing requirements or require that a collector register or certify their right to do business in the state.

THE MAGNITUDE OF CONSUMER DEBT

- ACA estimates that bad debt costs every man, woman, and child in the United States more than $269 per year. This means that a family of four would pay $1,076 more for goods and services during the year.
- On average, Americans write more than 1.7 million returned— or bounced—checks each day, totaling $51 million daily.
- As of September 1995, outstanding consumer debt totaled $995.1 billion, up more than $121 billion from September 1994, according to the Federal Reserve.
- According to the American Bankruptcy Institute, bankruptcy filings grew to 858,104 between June 1994 and June 1995, a 1.5 percent increase over the previous year. The American Bank-

ruptcy Institute attributes the increase to the consistent rise in consumer installment debt, which has steadily increased for twenty-five consecutive months.

- In 1990, 56 billion checks were processed and 482 million of those processed checks bounced. Projections for 1995 estimate that 72 billion checks will be processed and 619 million will bounce. Projections for the year 2000 estimate that 85 billion checks will be processed and 731 million of those checks will bounce.

THE ROLE OF ACA

- The American Collectors Association, Inc. (ACA) has 3,700 members in the United States and more than 50 other countries around the world.
- There are about 6,300 collection businesses in the United States.
- Members of ACA employ about 65,000.
- ACA members handle the collection of past-due retail, professional, and wholesale accounts receivable for one million commercial and consumer creditors.
- ACA members and their employees have access to 250 seminars a year for up-to-date training on collection regulations and techniques. ACA also administers certification and degree programs for advanced training in professional collections.

APPENDIX B: CHOOSING A PROFESSIONAL COLLECTION AGENCY

American Collectors Association, Inc.

Choosing a professional collection service to collect your delinquent accounts receivable requires careful consideration. The decision involves more than simply awarding your business to the lowest bidder, as the quality of the service you use will affect both your bottom line and your public image. Also, getting the most from using a collection firm requires mutual cooperation and good communication. Here are some factors to consider:

REFERENCES AND REPUTATION

Ask for at least two references, preferably in the same or similar business that you are in. If you're in a service business, look for clients in a service business. If you're selling retail merchandise, look for other businesses selling retail merchandise. Find out whether the firm has a good reputation in the community with merchants, other credit grantors, the Better Business Bureau, and the Chamber of Commerce.

MEMBERSHIP IN A TRADE ASSOCIATION

Look for membership in state and national trade associations such as the American Collectors Association, Inc. (ACA). Membership in ACA ensures that the firm has been screened by the organization before acceptance. Also, ACA members agree to adhere to the association's code of ethics, which covers client relationships as well as proper handling of consumers.

COMPLIANCE WITH LICENSING AND BONDING LAWS

Check whether the firm has complied with your state's licensing and/or bonding laws, if any. If state licensing or bonding is not required, check references and length of time the agency has been in business.

RATES AND RECOVERY PERCENTAGES

Rates and fees are usually charged on a contingency basis or on a combination of up-front fee and lower percentage. Selecting a collection firm solely on the rate it charges may not be the best decision. A firm that charges a low rate may not work your accounts as thoroughly and may collect on fewer of them. A firm that charges a higher rate may work accounts more thoroughly and recover more of them. The most important consideration for any creditor is the net return based on a combination of rate and recovery.

COLLECTION PROCEDURES AND POLICY

Ask what procedures the firm uses to collect, including when it would start work on your accounts after receiving them, the collection letters it uses, and whether it has trained telephone collectors and skiptracers. A visit to the collection office can be helpful, as you can observe the collection agency in operation. Ask about the office collection procedures and policies.

COLLECTOR TRAINING AND CERTIFICATION

What training do the firm's collectors receive? Are they educated in effective, professional collection techniques? Do they know how to comply with the federal Fair Debt Collection Practices Act (FDCPA)? Collectors who work for ACA members have access to educational materials and seminars covering all aspects of collections. ACA also conducts certification programs for collection professionals. Collectors can earn certification by successfully completing courses on the FDCPA and on professional telephone collectors' techniques and by passing a stringent exam.

REMITTANCE SCHEDULE AND REPORTING

Find out at what intervals the firm will be remitting funds to you that it has collected on your behalf. Also ask about account status reporting to find out what procedures and capabilities the firm offers.

SKIPTRACING AND FORWARDING

How does the collection firm locate debtors who can no longer be reached at the addresses or phone numbers listed on their accounts? Find out about the firm's skiptracing capabilities. Also, what are the firm's procedures regarding forwarding of accounts—the referral of accounts to another collection service in the locale to which a debtor has relocated? Members of ACA have access to a large forwarding network through ACA's Roster of 3,750 members.

SPECIAL SERVICES

Ask about client services that the collection firm may offer. Some firms offer client seminars or consultation on developing effective credit policies, precollection, and other credit and collection-related topics.

APPENDIX C: Q&A ABOUT DEBT COLLECTION

American Collectors Association, Inc.

WHAT IS A PROFESSIONAL DEBT COLLECTION SERVICE?

A professional debt collection service is a specialized business that collects past-due accounts for creditors. Professional debt collectors are third parties to the transaction that created the debt. They are collecting for the creditor but are not employees of the creditor. Sometimes third-party collectors are confused with creditors who have in-house departments collecting on their own behalf. The members of the American Collectors Association, Inc. are third-party collection offices.

WHAT'S THE DIFFERENCE BETWEEN A CREDITOR COLLECTING ON ITS OWN BEHALF AND A THIRD-PARTY COLLECTOR?

The collection practices of third-party collectors are directly regulated by the Fair Debt Collection Practices Act administered by the Federal Trade Commission. Credit grantor's collection practices are covered by law only under certain conditions. Also, third-party collection services are specifically set up for collection with specially trained staff and specialized equipment, including phone systems, computers, and collection software.

WHY ARE ACCOUNTS REFERRED FOR COLLECTION?

Most accounts are referred for collection because they have gone unpaid for a long time and the creditor has not received any communication from the consumer. People who provide goods and services to consumers on credit rely on their customers' promises to pay. While they value their customers, they must also depend on payment to meet their own expenses. The longer an account remains unpaid, the smaller the likelihood that it will be paid. When the creditor can no longer afford to carry past-due accounts and cannot collect them economically, the accounts are either written off or referred to professional, third-party collectors.

WHAT DOES A TYPICAL PROFESSIONAL COLLECTION OFFICE DO?

The collection service receives past-due accounts when those accounts cannot be collected economically by the creditor. Third-party collection services can collect many accounts more efficiently than creditors because their operations are streamlined and specialized for that purpose. Many times the collection service has to first find an accurate address or phone number so that they can contact the person who owes the account, a process called "skiptracing." After confirming the proper address, the office must include in a first written communication to the consumer a validation notice that allows him or her to dispute the validity of the debt and/or request verification of the debt.

Although exact procedures vary by collection office, type of account, and client, the consumer then receives a letter or phone call from a collector, who asks for payment in full. If payment in full is not possible, the collector works with the debtor to solve payment problems and make workable arrangements.

IS THERE A TYPICAL DEBTOR?

Collectors know that there is really no such thing as a typical debtor and that it's important to treat people according to their individual cases. Consumers from all walks of life can overextend themselves. Many have simply not planned their finances well. Still others have lost their jobs or suffered unexpected setbacks, such as accidents or illness.

WHAT ABOUT THOSE PEOPLE WHO HAVE FALLEN INTO DEBT BECAUSE OF CATASTROPHIC EVENTS, SUCH AS ACCIDENTS OR ILLNESS?

The American Collectors Association's Code of Ethics requires members to "show due consideration for the misfortunes of consumers in debt and to deal with them according to the merits of their individual cases." Collectors realize that they need to help such consumers find solutions for their financial difficulties and assist them in making plans to meet their financial obligations.

HOW CAN COLLECTORS CALL PEOPLE ABOUT THEIR DEBTS DAY IN AND DAY OUT?

Many people like working with other people, and that's exactly what a collector does—work with people. Collectors become experts in communication, especially in listening. Their work requires an understanding of human motivation and behavior. Because many credit grantors deal with large volumes of accounts receivable, often the collector is the first person to engage the consumer in a problem-solving dialogue about his or her unpaid bill. Collectors also enjoy the challenges and rewards of their job. A paid account represents success for the collector, recovery for his client, and peace of mind and self-respect for the consumer.

IS THE INDUSTRY REGULATED?

Collection practices are well-regulated by federal and state laws. The Fair Debt Collection Practices Act, administered by the Federal Trade Commission, prohibits abusive, misleading, and unfair debt collection practices.

HOW HAS THE COLLECTION INDUSTRY CHANGED OVER THE PAST FIFTEEN YEARS?

The biggest changes in the collection industry have resulted from increasing automation. Fifteen years ago, most collection offices kept track of accounts by using paper cards. Information was recorded manually and collectors dialed their phones themselves. Now, most offices are computerized and use collection-specific software. Sophisticated telephone systems with automated dialers are becoming common.

Also, collectors are better trained. The American Collectors Association, Inc. has an extensive education program for all aspects of the collection business. The association also administers certification and degree programs.

HOW IS THE COLLECTION INDUSTRY LIKELY TO CHANGE IN THE NEXT FIFTEEN YEARS?

Collection businesses are likely to offer more varied client services, including billing, accounts-receivable management, and storage of records using new optical scanning and storage devices.

HOW DOES BAD DEBT AFFECT THE ECONOMY?

According to the American Collectors Association, in the United States more than $70 billion is turned over to third-parties for collection annually. There is really no such thing as an unpaid bill. Those of us who do pay our bills ultimately pay for those who don't. Because bad debt represents an expense of doing business, it is partly offset by higher prices. The American Collectors Association estimates that each person in the United States pays $250 more for goods and services per year because of bad debt. Other consequences of nonpayment include business failures and the loss of jobs.

HOW DO THE EFFORTS OF THIRD-PARTY COLLECTORS AFFECT THE ECONOMY?

Third-party collectors reduce the amount of past-due accounts that are ultimately written off as bad debt. Collection, a part of accounts-receivable management, helps businesses maintain their cash flows and stay profitable. Collectors benefit consumers by helping to keep down the prices of goods and services. They also offer debtors an opportunity to talk with a person who can help them resolve payment problems without litigation. The collection industry itself employs about 125,000 people. Finally, the health of the U.S. economy depends on the proper functioning of the credit system, which gives consumers many choices. The collection industry is a necessary part of this credit system.

PART II:
THE TAXMAN AND THE LOTTERY: USING SETOFF PROGRAMS TO COLLECT OVERDUE ACCOUNTS

5 WILLIAMSBURG REGIONAL LIBRARY'S SETOFF PROGRAM

by Judith C. Fuss

WILLIAMSBURG REGIONAL LIBRARY
WILLIAMSBURG, VIRGINIA

SETTING THE STAGE

Every library has them—patron records with long overdue charges, a lost book or two. Despite all efforts to reclaim the materials and the charges due, there they sit, stubbornly defying all efforts at resolution. Overdue notices have been mailed—and returned as undeliverable. Reminder calls have been placed—to telephone numbers no longer current. Materials have been declared lost in the system and replacement charges added to records. No further action seems possible.

At the Williamsburg (Virginia) Regional Library, despite our low loss rate, we were frustrated by our inability to locate patrons who had long overdue charges and to recoup our losses. Supporting a significant student base, we found some students, upon graduation, leaving town with our books, CDs, or videos. When letters to a permanent address went unanswered, we found ourselves at a dead end. Other patrons moved frequently, leaving no forwarding address, and leaving the library little recourse. We examined and ruled out various collection-agency programs. These would have required significant changes to our policies with uncertain gain.

Then we learned that as a publicly funded institution we were eligible to participate in Virginia's Setoff Debt Collection Program, administered by the state's Department of Taxation. Through the program, authorized by state code in 1989, eligible institutions can collect on outstanding claims from taxpayers whom the state owes a refund for tax payments or lottery winnings. One-day hands-on training is provided free of charge by the Department of Taxation at their offices in Richmond for agency employees using the program. Step-by-step manuals lead the novice through the intricate maze of regulations, procedures, and deadlines. Though daunting at first, the program soon revealed itself to be a boon. Prompt and friendly support was readily available from Tax Department personnel every step of the way.

GETTING STARTED

We began preparing for our first year using setoff debt in the spring of 1994. Since our library operates under an independent board, we were to administer the program fully ourselves. Libraries that operate as a department of city government find many aspects handled by city offices. I was named to administer the program for the library as part of my other duties. We anticipated that less than one-half of my time averaged over the year, would be spent on the program. Through the summer, I determined the equipment I would need, drafted basic policies (see Figure 5.1), and tried to find out, by talking to others working with the program, how my life would change in January when matches started coming in.

The official *Setoff Debt User's Guide* was at once compact, straightforward, and totally confounding for a beginner like me. The intri-

---

FIGURE 5.1 Setoff Debt Collection Policies and Procedures

Williamsburg Regional Library
Setoff Debt Administrator
rev. 1/96

Setoff Debt Collection
Library Policies & Procedures

1. To be submitted for a claim, a record must be for an adult patron, contain a social security number, and have a balance of $10.00 or greater in fines or other charges owed to the library or arts center.
2. Claims will not be finalized for less than $5.00 unless the lesser amount clears the record.
3. Before finalizing a claim including replacement charges for paperbacks, the $3.00 processing fee should be waived for each paperback so as to be consistent with building procedures.
4. After a claim has been finalized, no changes shall be made to a record unless a library error is identified.
5. If, after a match but before finalization, a patron brings to the attention of the setoff debt administrator extenuating circumstances (e.g., card lost, though library not notified), then, at the discretion of the setoff debt administrator, the claim may be reduced by one-half.
6. If a claim is processed as paid by the state, then the patron pays the library directly for the same claim, the patron shall be refunded the amount paid by the state when such payment is received by the library.
7. When refunds are placed on a patron record, the setoff debt administrator will attempt to contact patron, notifying the patron of the refund, and requesting that they come to the library to receive payment. If the patron is not reachable by phone, or at the administrator's discretion, a request for refund form may be submitted to the Financial Assistant so that a check is prepared. The setoff debt administrator will mail the check to the patron along with a letter of explanation.

cate schedule of deadlines and time limits that must be adhered to precisely required several readings on my part to understand. It was not until I began working through real claims that the reason for each requirement became clear. The volume of paperwork looked unmanageable. Then I discovered that online access to setoff information through the State Tax Accounting and Reporting System (STARS) would allow me to add, change, delete, or reinstate claims without postal delays or more multicarbon forms. STARS also provided the opportunity to locate patrons' social security numbers and current addresses in the tax database when this information was missing or incorrect in our patron records. Locating this information enabled me to submit claims that otherwise would not have been accepted for submission.

To get online, we needed an IBM-compatible PC loaded with ProComm Plus and connected to a modem. The cost to the library would be long distance phone charges to Richmond while operating online. A script provided on disk by STARS and loaded on to the designated PC would perform automatic dial up and log on, and program certain computer keys for setoff functions. We signed up for STARS and I began setting up our workstation, using an existing PC and modem, shared at that time with another part-time library staff person.

We defined the parameters of the claims we would submit. Each claim had to have a social security number, which is the identifying element for verifying a match between a claim and available funds. Library staff have been requesting individual social security numbers as part of patron registrations for approximately five years, although it is not required for a library card. Most adult patron records contained this. Using STARS, we would be able to obtain some social security numbers not listed or correct numbers when invalid ones had been provided. We also decided that claims would be submitted for adult patrons only. Our patron records are designated Adult, Young Adult, or Children. While significant outstanding charges exist on young adults' and children's records, the likelihood of these individuals being due a refund of state tax monies or lottery winnings was slim. The time required to manage these claims would outweigh any return. The state does not allow claims of less than $5.00 to be submitted; we established a claim cut-off value of $10.00. This amount represents the estimated value of staff time to handle a claim plus actual costs, such as paper and postage. For a claim to be submitted, the patron must owe $10.00 or more for such things as overdue fines, replacement or damage charges, or room rentals. Using these parameters, I was able to draft a recall program which extracted a list of patron records from our Dynix automated system. We were on our way.

The next step was to get these claims into the tax-system database, to be matched. We were able to purchase a customized program, previously developed by Dynix for Hampton (Virginia) Public Library, to transfer this data to tape in a format that could be submitted directly to the Department of Taxation. The transfer took less than an hour and provided us with just over 1,400 records to submit; of these, over 1,100 were entered as valid claims. The remaining social security numbers either were not found in the tax system or did not match the taxpayer name as submitted. Incorrect social security numbers were later corrected and the claims submitted through STARS. The proportion of selected records to valid claims, approximately 79 percent, has remained consistent throughout the year.

When we first began to submit claims, the tax-system database was cleared of setoff claims each year in late fall. Participating agencies had to resubmit all claims yearly. Beginning in November, claims were entered into the database on a first-received basis. The earlier a claim was submitted, the lower its assigned tax claim number and the higher the claim priority. If several claims were submitted for one taxpayer and a match was later made, the claim with the lowest claim number would be satisfied first. Claims were not accepted by the Department of Taxation before November 1 for the following claim year, but could be submitted throughout the year. Of course, it was to an agency's advantage to submit the bulk of its claims as soon after November 1 as possible. In summer 1994, the department changed this procedure in response to agency requests, and all outstanding claims existing in the system are now automatically rolled over as of January 1 to the next year. This allows older claims to retain a higher priority and reduces the volume of claims submitted each year.

MATCHING CLAIMS

To identify matches, the Department of Taxation's computer compares submitted tax returns with outstanding claims. When a match is made, a precise schedule of notification and reply is set in motion. The department notifies the agency by mailed computer printout that a match has been made listing the claimant's name and address as it appears on the most recent tax return, social security number, claim number, and amount of match. The agency has ten days to verify the claim by checking its records and notify the patron. If notification is not accomplished within ten days, the agency must forfeit the claim.

The Department of Taxation has a series of forms for notification. Each agency must develop the forms and letters it will use. The letter the Williamsburg Regional Library uses to notify patrons of a match is shown in Figure 5.2. The amount of the match represents monies available at the time the match is made and may not fully satisfy the claim. This may be all the taxpayer is due, or other agencies may have previously matched funds. In our example (Figure 5.2), Minnie owes the library $35.90, but the match is for $22.90. After the library receives this money from the state, Minnie will still owe the library $13.00.

FIGURE 5.2 Patron-Notification Letter

January 2, 1998

Minnie Mae Mouse
1 Sleeping Beauty Lane
Orlando, FL 11224

2 1688 00012 3456

Dear Minnie Mouse:

Library records show that you have outstanding charges on the library card listed above in the amount of $35.90. By authority of the Code of Virginia, Sections 58.1-520 through 58.1-534, this account has been forwarded to the Commonwealth of Virginia Department of Taxation Setoff Debt Collection Program for recovery. A match of this claim, with tax refund monies or lottery winnings due you, has been made in the amount of $22.90, and will be applied to your library debt.

If you feel there has been a mistake concerning the validity of this claim and you wish to contest in an administrative hearing, you must notify the Library in writing of your intent within 30 days of the postmark date on this letter. Send written notice of contest to

        Judith C. Fuss
        Williamsburg Regional Library
        515 Scotland Street
        Williamsburg, VA 23185

If written notice is not received, your opportunity to contest is automatically waived.

If you have any questions about this claim, please contact me at 220-9216. Do not contact the Virginia Department of Taxation, as they have no information about this claim.

Yours truly,

Judith C. Fuss
Setoff Debt Administrator

Along with the letter, I send a screen print of the charges (see Figure 5.3), which provides titles and due dates for outstanding materials.

FIGURE 5.3 Screen Print of Charges

```
                        Williamsburg Regional Library
                                Circulation

CHECKOUT & RENEWAL

MOUSE, MINNIE MAE     2 1688 00012 3456        55555

# Overdue =    0     # Lost =   0     $ Due =     $35.90

# REASON                 TITLE                          DUEDATE       BAL
Charges - misc. fees  Minorities, a changing role in   04 APR 97   $23.95
Charges - misc. fees  The mugging of Black America     04 APR 97   $11.95
```

Providing this additional detail has greatly reduced the number of calls for information about claims and also has aided in the return of materials. One video, part of a series of Shakespeare's plays each valued at over $98.00, was returned after two years. The patron explained that seeing the type and title of the item helped him locate the tape.

The taxpayer has thirty days from the date of the notification letter in which to respond to the agency. All questions go to the agency, as the Department of Taxation does not know details of particular claims. Most inquiries we receive are about the transactions that led to the charges. Usually a review of checkout dates, titles, and types of materials resolves the questions. Sometimes the patron still has the items and wants to return them. If they are returned in circulating condition, the charges are reduced to the maximum charge for each item type ($5.00 each for books, CDs, or audio tapes; $10.00 each for videos). Patrons may pay the library directly or allow the charges to be taken out of their tax refund. If the patron pays the library in full, I immediately delete the claim from the setoff database through STARS access.

A recurring situation prompted an adjustment to our initial setoff policy. A patron explains that he had lost his library card (or it was stolen) several years ago, but never reported this to the library. He says the items in question were checked out after the card was stolen and therefore he should not be responsible for the charges. Since the loss of the card was never reported to the library and the card remained active, under library policy associated charges are still the responsibility of the patron. With a setoff match in place and the charges valid, the library is entitled to collect the match despite possible mitigating circumstances. To defuse such awkward situations, we adopted a policy allowing us to meet the patron half-way by waiving half of the charges, with the patron responsible for half. Patrons have responded positively to this compromise.

If a patron feels that a claim is invalid and cannot resolve the issue with the agency, the claim may be contested in an administrative hearing. A request for a hearing must be made in writing to the agency within the thirty-day period. If written notice is not received, the patron's opportunity to contest is automatically waived. A hearing addresses only the validity of the claim. It does not deal with internal policies of the agency that led to the charges or the way in which the policies were carried out. Such matters must be handled directly between the agency and the taxpayer outside the context of the setoff debt program. During our three years of participation, we have never had a claim contested.

Once the patron has been notified, I add a Clarify with Supervisor message to the library record, noting that a match has been made and the patron notified. The message will appear each time the patron's record is accessed. The Clarify with Supervisor message is rarely used by library staff for other purposes, so it is a flag that a setoff match is in place. Circulation staff have been trained (see Figure 5.4) to look for this message. If a patron pays setoff charges at the circulation desk, staff processes the payment, then forwards the ID number of the patron record and the amount paid to me. If payment satisfies the claim and clears all charges from the record, I delete the claim from the setoff database through STARS. If charges still remain on the record, I allow the claim to stand against future matches. If the claim is satisfied but cannot be deleted because payment is in process, the library sends a refund from the state to the patron when that payment is received (see Refunding Duplicate Payments, p. 70).

FINALIZING CLAIMS

The taxpayer is allowed thirty days to contact the agency and resolve any questions about the charges. During that time, the amount of the match is held by the Department of Taxation, pending finalization of the claim. After thirty days, I check the record again and if the claim has not been resolved directly with the library, I use STARS online access to authorize payment from the state. If items have been returned or there are extenuating circumstances that have been brought to my attention so that charges on the record have been reduced, the claim

---

FIGURE 5.4 Training Memo to Circulation Staff

MEMO

TO: Circ Assistants

FROM: Judy Fuss

Subject: Setoff Debt: What Should I Do?

Date: March 13, 1995

Now that the realities of the setoff debt program are coming to meet us face to face, a few words on specifics might be of help to you. Rosemary has allowed me some time at your next Circ meeting to give an overview and answer questions. This memo will supplement.

<u>**Dealing With Setoff Cases**</u>

Look and listen for the following clues to the "setoff connection."
1. A "Clarify with Supervisor" message on a patron record. Look for "Notification of setoff match mailed" on the detail screen.
2. Patron says, "I received a letter saying . . ." in combination with any of the following:
   "...I owe the library money."
   "...the library is taking my tax refund."
   "...the state says I never returned books."
3. The words state or tax in combination with questions about money the patron owes the library.

If you suspect a setoff connection, refer the patron to me.

If the patron wishes to return items and/or pay fines and you suspect a setoff connection, handle the transaction, then forward the patron's ID # to me for review and adjustment of setoff claim.

Refer any patron questions about setoff, either by phone or in person, to me.

<u>**Tightening Procedures**</u>

Now that we are actively pursuing unpaid debts through this program, it is really important that we follow our own procedures meticulously. Please be careful about the following:

1. Shelf Checks
   Now that overdue notification is handled by phone, the shelf list relates to final notices only. This means that routine shelf checks for overdue items is no longer being done. Audrey & Susan are checking the shelves for those items which generate final notices. Please be diligent about filling out shelf check slips when patrons request this or if they comment that they returned an item.

FIGURE 5.4 (cont.)

---

2. **Modifying Patron Records**
   When changing an address or other information on a patron record without the library card present, be extremely careful that you have the right record on the screen. Verify the correct record by checking factors such as social security number, previous address, telephone number. This is critical when there are multiple listings for the same or similar names.

3. **Checking Out Materials Using Patron ID**
   Double check that you have the correct record before checking items out for a patron using ID. If more than one name similar to the one for which you are searching exists on the index, verify the correct record by checking several factors such as social security number, address, etc.

4. **Check for a Duplicate Card**
   When issuing a "new" card to a patron, carefully check for an existing record. If a record already exists with charges on it, this provides an opportunity of notifying the patron of these.

5. **Ask for Social Security Number**
   If no social security number is listed on a record, ask if we may list it. Most of our records now do have SSNs, but the more listed, the easier for me.

---

is finalized for the lesser amount. Once a claim has been finalized, it cannot be deleted from the setoff database.

Some patrons, once contacted, will want to resolve the matter quickly. If they are unable to pay the library directly, they may authorize me to finalize the claim immediately rather than waiting the full thirty days.

When a claim has been finalized, I add a note under the Clarify with Supervisor block on the patron record as payment can now be sent to the library.

RECEIVING PAYMENT

Once a month the state sends setoff payments for finalized claims to participating agencies through electronic funds transfer. At the beginning of each month, a report of payments is mailed to the setoff debt coordinator in each agency, listing taxpayer name, address, claim number and claim amount. Using this report, I record payment on library records.

The state deducts an administrative fee for each claim paid, equal to 4 percent of the match. I waive this amount from the patron's record after payment has been posted. If the match does not satisfy the claim, the administrative fee is not waived at the time of the first match. For example, Mickey Mouse owes the library $21.00 for a book that has been declared lost. The setoff claim for this amount has been matched in full ($21.00). The library receives payment of $20.16, which is posted to Mickey's record. The remaining $.84, representing the state's administrative fee, is waived as it is too small to submit again as a claim. However, Minnie Mouse owes the library $35.90 for two lost books, and her claim is matched for $22.90. The library receives payment of $21.98, which is posted to her record. The remaining balance of $13.92 is allowed to stand, pending future matches or payment.

REFUNDING DUPLICATE PAYMENTS

Although patrons have thirty days between the time of a match and finalization of the claim to contact the library, resolve any questions, return library materials, or explain extenuating circumstances that might reduce the amount of the claim, sometimes they wait until after the claim has been finalized to call or come in. After a claim has been finalized, charges will be reduced only if materials are returned in circulating condition or if library error in establishing the charges is identified. If a claim has been finalized, it cannot be deleted from or reduced on the Department of Taxation database because payment is in process. The payment will be sent to the library in accordance with the finalization notice. If the patron pays the library directly for the claim, the payment is noted on the patron's record. Then if duplicate payment is received from the state (anywhere from a few days to six weeks later, depending on when in the schedule patron payment is received), the library gives the patron a refund since otherwise the library would be receiving duplicate payment.

If I discover that payment has previously been posted to the record of a patron for whom I have received payment from the state, I add a credit in the amount of the refund due to the record, then submit a refund request to the library's financial department. A check is prepared which I mail, with a letter of explanation (Figure 5.5), after posting the refund to the patron's record.

FIGURE 5.5 Refund Letter to Patron

[date]

[name]
[street]
[city state zip]

[barcode]

Dear [fullname]

You recently paid the library for charges which were outstanding on the library card listed above. These charges had been submitted to the Commonwealth of Virginia Department of Taxation's Setoff Debt Collection Program for recovery. The library received payment for this claim from the Virginia Department of Taxation after receiving your payment. Enclosed please find a refund in the amount of $[amount] from the library.

We appreciate your support of the library.

If you have any questions about this matter, please contact me at 220-9216.

Yours truly,

Judith C. Fuss
Setoff Debt Administrator

PROGRAM RESULTS

The library has been participating in the Setoff Debt Collection Program for three years. The program has shown itself to be an effective method of gaining payment for long-overdue charges and receiving back some library materials thought irretrievably lost. Looking at the first year in rounded numbers, we submitted over 1,300 claims valued at $50,000. A total of $7,242 was collected in payments from the state or directly from patrons in response to notification of a setoff match. A 4 percent administrative fee on each match paid is retained by the state to cover their costs in running the program. This totaled $250 for our first year. $508 worth of library materials were recovered. Of the claims submitted, just under 25 percent were matched and paid. The claims not matched remain in the setoff database and have been rolled over to the 1996 collection year. About 21 percent of patron records selected from the system as fulfilling our setoff criteria cannot be entered as claims because the patron is not on the tax rolls. This profile has remained generally consistent over our three years' participation. In 1996, the library collected almost $6,500; 1997 brought in over $6,700.

Less than 20 percent of my time, averaged over the year, is spent administering this program. The time spent drops each year, as I become more accustomed to the program's routine. April is the peak month, when close to 40 percent of my time may be spent on setoff matters. No equipment purchases were needed to implement the program or to gain STARS access. In spring of 1994 we purchased custom programming ($500), a one-time expense, to streamline the transfer of claims to the state's setoff database. At that time the only other method of transfer was by using cumbersome paper forms. Changes to the program in 1996, allowing claims to be carried over from year to year in the tax department's system and online claim entry, made subsequent use of this programming obsolete. Other costs were telephone charges to add, delete, and finalize claims online and paper and postage for notification and refund letters. For a $900 outlay our first year, we received over $7,000 in return. These were charges that had defied our usual collection attempts—three phone calls, notifying of overdue materials, and a mailed notice of replacement charges when the materials were declared lost. The largest numbers of matches were made in March and April, with the bulk of payments received in May and June.

PUBLIC RESPONSE

The program was begun without a lot of publicity. Short articles (see Figure 5.6) appeared in the local newspaper and in the library's monthly newsletter, after the program was under way. These generated a few positive comments from patrons who praised our efforts to reclaim outstanding debts.

The city and county governments, which provide the bulk of our funding, and our governing library board were highly supportive. Personnel administering the program for the county were very helpful in sharing information about day-to-day operation and their in-house procedures.

Response from patrons whose tax refunds are matched through the program have been surprisingly supportive. Most of those who contact me are chagrined that they have library debts they had forgotten and are all too willing to resolve the claim quickly. I even received a

FIGURE 5.6 Article appearing in *The Virginia Gazette* 4/19/95

WILLIAMSBURG—The regional library has found a way to reclaim its overdue books: have the tax man ask for them. As a local government service, the library qualifies for reimbursements through the state Department of Taxation's Set-Off Debt Collection program. Through its computerized program, the state checks its list of those qualifying for tax refunds or lottery winnings against a list of unpaid debts claimed by government agencies. If a match is made and no debt to another agency has priority, the library may receive a part or all of the money owed to it. The library's outstanding debt total reflects fines and fees accrued for several years on library materials and Arts Center rentals. The library tries to avoid increasing patron debt by use of its electronic telephone notification system that notifies patrons of overdue materials three times over a seven-week period. Most books are returned when patrons are reminded of their status. However, outstanding debts include more than 1,000 patron claims, or more than $42,000. By mid-March more than $3,300 worth of those claims had been matched by the state Department of Taxation. The library stands to reclaim more than $40,000 in lost community property and fines through the program. And the tax man doesn't have to call twice.

letter from a woman thanking me for pursuing her claim, which was more than two years old. She had moved out of the area, not realizing that the charges remained unpaid. She remembered our library fondly and was glad to lend her support. Some contacts led to the return of materials, sometimes packed away in storage, sometimes just overlooked. Only one response was confrontational.

SUMMARY

After three years, I can unequivocally say that the program has been effective and worthwhile. Not only do we receive between $6,000 and $7,000 each year that would not have come to the library in any other way, but we also recover materials thought to be gone forever. Once I became practiced at the program's rhythms, I found that it did not require as much of my time as I had anticipated. I developed a system of tracking claims and payments using a PC database. This is a safeguard against library error or duplication and allows me to retrieve yearly statistics. Taxes may be universally abhorred. But I have found that, in some cases, the tax man can be a friend.

THE HAMPTON PUBLIC LIBRARY SETOFF PROGRAM

by Sharon Winters

PIERCE COUNTY LIBRARY
TACOMA, WASHINGTON

The installation of an integrated automated library system in 1987 provided the Hampton (Virginia) Public Library System with its first reliable data about overdue rates. During the late 1980s and early 1990s, a period of flat and sometimes reduced budget allocations, the library staff made numerous attempts to reduce overdue rates in order to increase the availability of materials. Loan periods and fine rates were altered, and an electronic phone notification system was installed to make more frequent customer contact with those who had overdue materials. Bookmarks and posters were distributed to increase awareness of loan periods, fine rates, and the importance of returning materials in a timely manner so they might be available to others in the community. Over a five-year period, these methods reduced overdue rates from 24 percent to of all materials in circulation to 18 percent.

While gradually realizing a reduction in overdue rates, the library also wanted to retrieve materials that had passed into long overdue, or "lost," status. The library's annual loss rate was less than 0.75 percent, but this meant 3,500-4,500 items a year. During the late 1980s the library system made a number of generally unsuccessful and labor-intensive attempts to collect long overdue library materials through civil court proceedings. Library administrators also explored the possibility of using a debt collection agency but decided that the expense and tactics were not appropriate to the task. Library users, frustrated when denied access to materials retained by others, occasionally questioned library staff about what means were being taken to retrieve long overdue materials. Library staff, concerned with being good stewards of tax-supported library resources and desiring increased availability of a somewhat limited collection, were equally frustrated.

Fortunately in 1990 the City of Hampton became involved in a statewide program intended to address the very problem faced by the library: how to collect bad debts owed governmental agencies. The library quickly joined the initiative, the Commonwealth of Virginia's "Setoff Debt" program. The program, enacted in similar form in other states, allows state agencies, the courts, and municipalities to collect outstanding fines and fees by debiting state income tax refunds and state lottery prize winnings. Delinquent fines and fees totalling as little as $5 per agency can be submitted to the state's Department of Taxation; when a person files for a state income tax refund or wins a state lottery prize, the debt is withheld from the refund or prize winnings and forwarded to the agency. The program is part of state law: the Setoff Debt Collection Act, effective June 1989. From 1993 through 1995, the initiative allowed the City of Hampton to collect $475,000 for delinquent personal property taxes, traffic tickets, library fees and other delinquent fees.

DEVELOPMENT OF THE PROGRAM

Before the library entered the program in 1990, patron registration records were altered to include a field for social security number, which is required in all records submitted to the Setoff Debt program. During a four-month effort, staff collected and added social security numbers to the registration records of most active adult and juvenile library users. Under state law, Virginia citizens cannot be required to provide their social security numbers, but library staff encountered little resistance to their requests, especially after explaining the purpose.

Library staff define criteria for inclusion in the Setoff Debt program. Customers with $10 or more in fines or charges for unreturned materials are included, though the state allows inclusion at the $5 level. (Because of limits on the maximum overdue fine per item, the vast majority of people included in the program are those who have not returned library materials. The library charges the retail price of the item plus a $5 processing fee for each unreturned item.) Juveniles (under age eighteen), are excluded from the program, though their social security numbers are collected at the time of registration. However, letters are sent to parents notifying them of excessive fine balances at the beginning of tax season. In Virginia, debts of minor children are the fiscal responsibility of the parent or guardian, though charges accrued by juvenile patrons cannot be debited from the income tax refunds of a parent or guardian.

To keep costs low, library administrators decided to automate the data gathering for the Setoff Debt program using the library's Dynix system. Working with Hampton's systems librarian and a member of the city data processing staff, a Dynix programmer designed software that creates a file of customers meeting the above criteria and transfers that file to magnetic tape. Tape data includes the crucial social security number, name, address, city/state/zip, amount due, and customer barcode number. The software was originally designed as custom programming for Hampton Public Library, but is now marketed as a Dynix product by Ameritech Library Services, based in Provo, Utah.

THE PROCESS

In October of each year the library sends a tape to the city data processing department, which compiles data from participating city departments. A master tape is sent to the Virginia Department of Taxation in early November, which ensures that Hampton will be among the first in the queue of state, city, and court agencies to receive money debited from state income tax refunds and lottery prize winnings. At the beginning of tax season in early January, the library starts sending monthly tapes to the city data processing department, revising data as customers return or pay for materials and are added to or deleted from the list. It takes about fifteen minutes to create the file and less than two minutes to dump the file to tape. During the 1994 tax season, a typical tape included 5,750 library users who met the criteria for inclusion from a file of 95,000 registered borrowers. Income of $16,000 was received from just 741 taxpayers during the library's 1995 fiscal year. Debts are recovered from less than 15 percent of the names submitted because juveniles are excluded, many people who file are not due refunds, and some people move out of state before clearing their library debt. Records of fines are retained by the library for at least five years, so the same library users appear in the file year-after-year until they pay the fine or file for a state income tax refund that can be debited.

When a customer who has been included on the tape files for a state income tax refund, the state notifies the city which, within seven days, sends a letter notifying the taxpayer of the library's claim against their refund (see Figure 6.1). The letter includes a library contact name and phone number. The customer has thirty days to respond by returning the materials or paying the fee directly to the library, in which case the library contacts the city's Setoff Debt coordinator to clear the record with the Department of Taxation. Regardless of the customer's action, the portion of their income tax refund which the library is trying to collect is held for thirty days. (If the refund due is less than the fees due, the library collects a partial payment and retains the balance in its customer "block" files.) The state also adds a 4 percent processing charge, so a customer who owes the library $100 would have $104 debited. Until the debt is cleared, either through direct payment, return of the item, or transfer of funds from the state to the city to the library, the customer is barred from using his or her library card. (Library users are blocked from checkout if their fines and/or fees total $2 or more.)

If an income tax refund is debited, the money is transferred to the library's book and subscriptions budget, a process which takes thirty to forty-five days to complete. Working from a printout of collected

---

FIGURE 6.1   Notification Letter to Taxpayer

City of Hampton, Virginia
Hampton Public Libraries
4207 Victoria Blvd.
Hampton, VA 23669
October 4, 1993

                                          SSN

Setoff Debt Collection Account:

According to our records you have a library fine of $00.00. A tax refund due a taxpayer may be applied against any delinquent indebtedness owed the City pursuant to the **Setoff Debt Collection Act, Section 58.1-520 et seq of the *Code of Virginia*.** This is to advise you that $ of your refund has been delayed and assigned to the City to be applied against your unpaid account.

We must receive written notification in this office within thirty days (30) from the date of this letter informing us that you intend to contest the validity of this claim. If you fail to apply for a hearing in writing within the thirty day (30) period, it will be deemed a waiver of the opportunity to contest the claim causing final Setoff by default. We will then direct the Virginia Department of Taxation to transfer the above amount, which includes a Virginia Department of Taxation handling fee, to the City of Hampton.

The Virginia Department of Taxation is not responsible for handling inquiries concerning this debt. If you have questions concerning the validity of the debt, or if you wish to pay the accounts in order to release your refund, please call:

> **Hampton Public Library**
> **Marian Simmons (809) 727-1154**

                    Yours truly,

                    Delores F. Adams
                    Setoff Debt Coordinator

debts, a staff member manually clears customer "block" screens, adding a note that the fine or fee has been collected through the Setoff Debt program. Occasionally a customer returns the item(s) or pays the library directly after his or her income tax refund has been debited. In those cases, the library refunds the amount debited based on information obtained from the city's Setoff Debt coordinator. The $5 per item processing fee is retained by the library if the item is returned after the library has received the funds from the state.

IMPACT ON STAFF

In preparation for joining the Setoff Debt program, library staff did shelf checks for all materials checked out to seven hundred customers with a large number of unreturned materials. Very few items were located, which gave staff confidence in the library's check-in procedures and the record-keeping that could lead to a customer being included in the program. There have been few instances in which the library's information was incorrect. (The city has established hearing procedures for appeals under the Setoff Debt Collection Act.)

Because data is gathered just once a month during tax season, it is quite possible for materials to be returned after a tape is cut but before a notification letter is received. During the height of the tax season, three staff members spend an average of three hours per week responding to such customer queries, reviewing library records with city staff at the thirty-day point, clearing blocks once monies have been received, and issuing refunds. From reports provided by the city's Setoff Debt coordinator, staff also clean up library registration records for name changes, address corrections, and duplicate social security numbers.

The senior library assistant responsible for day-to-day operations of the library's automated system manages the program with assistance from a staff member in the circulation department and the library's administrative assistant. Staff with circulation responsibilities are reminded of procedures at the beginning of each tax season, so they can expeditiously refer queries to the senior library assistant. The following case study is particularly helpful in outlining the process to staff so they can explain it to customers.

OVERDUES MANAGEMENT AND THE SETOFF DEBT PROGRAM: A CASE STUDY

1. Electronic phone notification system contacts customers about overdue materials at seven, fourteen, and forty days past due. Data mailers generated by the Dynix software are mailed at twenty-one days past due. Customers are billed for the item at sixty days past due and blocked from checkout.
2. "Notice of outstanding fines" is sent to all customers with fines or fees exceeding $25.
3. During tax season, the library sends monthly tapes with data on customers with $10 or more in fines or fees.
4. Terry Tardy files for a state income tax refund in the amount of $100 on March 1.
5. Terry's refund request is matched against files for state, court, and city agency claims for delinquent debts. Terry owes the library $20 for unreturned library materials. The state notifies the city that Terry is due a refund, but that $20 will be held. Within seven days the city sends a notification letter to Terry indicating that she has thirty days to respond.
6. In late March, the state issues Terry a partial-refund check for $79.20 ($100 minus the $20 she owes the library and $.80 [4 percent of total] retained by the state as a processing charge).
7. Terry fails to return the overdue materials or pay the $20 directly to the library.
8. In May the library receives a list of taxpayers whose income tax refunds will be debited. The library manually checks block screens to be sure nothing has cleared since the last data tape was sent to city hall. Indeed, Terry still has not returned her materials.
9. In late May, Terry's state income tax refund is officially debited by $20.80, so she does not receive the balance of her refund. The library receives a list of customers from whom it will receive money and deducts the amount received from their block screens. The $20 Terry owes is transferred from the state to the city and into the library's book and subscriptions budget in late May or early June.
10. Three months later Terry Tardy finds the unreturned item and decides to return it. The library retains a $5 processing charge and issues Terry a refund check for the balance.

RESULTS

With a tax-filing deadline of May 1, most income is received by the library between April and July. Funds deposited into the book and subscriptions budget allow librarians to order replacements, especially in the adult nonfiction collection, which suffers the highest loss rate. Because it has proven difficult to project Setoff Debt income in advance and most funds are received at the end of the fiscal year, much of the income is devoted to special projects. Projects are identified by collection development staff in the early spring and desiderata lists are compiled. Recent initiatives include a dramatic addition to the bookmobile's juvenile collection, PC workstations to support CD Rom products, and updating of the library's science collections.

The library has participated in the Setoff Debt program for five years, generally seeing increases in income each year, except during a period when there were problems with the Department of Taxation's software (see Figure 6.2).

FIGURE 6.2 Income from Setoff Debt Program 1991–1995		
Fiscal Year	**Income from State**	**Refunds to Customers**
1991	$4700	$300
1992	$4400	$400
1993	$3000	$500
1994	$9700	$700
1995	$16000	$550
Total Income after Refunds	$35,350	

Though the income is certainly a boon to the budget, staff are equally heartened by the knowledge that many long overdue materials are returned when customers receive the letters warning of imminent reductions to their state income tax refunds. As each year's filing deadline approaches, staff more frequently see the Dynix check-in message, "Hey! We just found a LOST item." Because it is impossible to know how many items are returned as a result of the letter, library staff cannot place a dollar value on materials retrieved but know that the Setoff Debt program has a significant impact on the library's long-term loss rate.

Customers applaud the library's efforts to seek means, beyond the traditional overdue notice, to retrieve materials purchased with tax-payer funds. During the second year of the library's participation in the Setoff Debt program, a customer who had been included unwittingly provided the library with some free publicity about the initiative. The customer had several long overdue library materials and filed at the beginning of the tax season, expecting a speedy refund. Angered by the withholding of a portion of his refund check, he contacted the local newspaper which ran a page-one story, complete with color photo of the grimacing customer. Fortunately, the reporter interviewed library and city staff about the program in order to explain its purpose. The publication of the article caused a small deluge of returns of overdue materials.

CONCLUSION

Instead of accepting a certain materials loss rate as the "cost of doing business," libraries should seek opportunities to recover long overdue material. Automated library systems provide the information and the tools to retrieve these materials. Programs in Kansas, Minnesota, and other states, similar to Virginia's Setoff Debt program, provide the means.

In evaluating methods of retrieving these materials, a library must weigh the costs against the benefits. The low cost of Hampton Public Library's involvement in the Setoff Debt program is key to its success. One-time expenses totalled $500 for the software, while ongoing costs primarily involve the three hours of staff time devoted to the program each week during the four-month tax season. The support of the city's Setoff Debt coordinator and data processing staff centralizes much of the program management, to the advantage of participating city departments. The benefits, in terms of materials returned and the recovery of thousands of dollars in charges for unreturned materials, are significant. Such efforts also send a message to those who retain materials that library resources are valued resources.

7 THE AXE LIBRARY SETOFF PROGRAM

by Susan M. Johns

AXE LIBRARY AND
PITTSBURG STATE UNIVERSITY

Delinquent patrons: how many times have we as librarians thought, "If they'd just return the books on time, none of this would have to happen"? Setoff procedures are usually the last in a series of steps to re-claim lost materials and recover funds for fines, damaged items, and replacement copies. The costs are real in terms of frustration, paperwork, time, and effort. Those of us with automated library systems tend to assume automation is faster, but our systems often present many pitfalls.

This chapter examines the use of automated data in the setoff process, describes the steps used by one university campus, and considers various options when implementing or maintaining setoff processes.

PHILOSOPHICAL BEGINNINGS

Seriously delinquent patron accounts are the basis of all setoff collection procedures. We may have a pile of overdue cards, or we may work our way up from the "bottom line" of a printout listing warrants, or it may take the form of an interagency body associated with state legal departments. Based on recovery charges, use of staff time, and success rates, each avenue of debt collection has good points and bad.

The common thread of debt collection, regardless of the agency or business implementing the setoff procedures for the library, is the data provided by the library to that particular agency or business. Roger Mendelson, in his article, "A Simple Guide to Solving Your Book Return Problem," writes about five procedural areas that, from the standpoint of a collection agency, are critical to the success of debt recovery. These are 1) obtaining proper patron information; 2) checking the patron information for accuracy and validity; 3) making borrower's rights and responsibilities known; 4) establishing consistent procedures of follow-up once a debt is incurred; and 5) turning over the debt to a competent collection agency.

Most libraries assume they do a fairly good job at the steps outlined above. In reality, all of us could probably do a lot better. For instance, when obtaining proper ID, how much incorrect data is a result of bad handwriting on library card applications? We may say we verify applications against a driver's license or utility bill, but why is it that the post office recognizes these people as "unknown" almost immediately and the address stated as a vacant lot? We may require the patron to sign an application form, we may even charge for a patron card, but does the patron really read the application form and understand the policies of our library? Since we keep the copy of the application that clearly states the library rules and penalties, are our patrons not entitled to a copy of this "contract"? Are our policies clear in signage, on bookmarks, or on overdue notices, or are we guilty of "oversignage" and too much information?

Do our overdue notices convey progressively stronger intent in their wording? Are our policies of notification and appeal consistent, timely, and methodical? Are we too lenient? How much time do we allow to lapse—time for patrons to move, semesters to end, books to disappear in moving cartons? Finally, do we have the necessary data to turn the debt over to an outside agency with minimal disruption of our staff and their time?

THE STATE OF KANSAS SETOFF PROGRAM : AN EXAMPLE

Pittsburg State University, along with approximately sixty other State of Kansas agencies, is eligible to refer delinquent patron accounts to the Kansas Department of Revenue under Kansas Statutes #75-6201 and #75-6205. The criteria for submission is fairly straightforward: " . . . the debt must be owed to the State agency/municipality, the debt must be considered delinquent, and for municipalities, at least three attempts must have been made to collect the debt prior to its submission." In addition, KSA (Kansas Statutes Annotated) #75-6205 sets a minimum debt amount of at least $25 for any debt submitted.

The Kansas Setoff Program matches patron information submitted by the library against various state payments, including payroll, state income tax refunds, homestead property tax and food sales tax, as well as payments coming from retirement contributions (KPERS), unemployment insurance, and Kansas Lottery winnings. In addition, library debt can also be set off against a percentage of court-ordered child support payments.

Once the delinquent patron data is turned over to the state (in either electronic or paper format), the Setoff Program begins the process of matching library data against the patron's social security number. Notices are sent out directly from the state describing the debt, rights to an administrative appeal, and procedures for clearing the debt. When the debt is collected, the patron receives a receipt from the state, and the setoff money is paid back to the home agency less a 17 percent collection fee.

THE ROLE OF THE LIBRARY IN THE SETOFF PROCESS

Pittsburg State University's (PSU) Axe Library is but one small cog in the state setoff process. A great deal of work goes on during setoff "season," if you will, that reflects efforts throughout the year. The efforts regularly include evaluation of the loan code and circulation policies, blocking of patron privileges, diligent record keeping, tracking addresses for return-requested envelopes, and liberal doses of patience, note-taking, and stacks searching.

LOAN CODE POLICY

Adjustments to the loan code were made before major setoff efforts began. The new loan code reflected an underlying philosophical principle that we were not in the setoff business to make money, but to get material returned back into the collection and avoid repurchasing titles. The code was modified so that the average patron (with a three-week or twenty-one-day checkout) would receive one overdue notice when items become overdue, a final overdue notice 3 weeks later, and after 6 weeks an automatic billing notice. The billing notice indicates that the item is assumed lost and billed according to current market prices, whenever possible. In addition, a fourth notice goes out for any amount over $10 as notification of a hold placed against transcript requests or continued enrollment at the university.

The policy of looking up each bibliographic item in BIP+ or Baker and Taylor Link is rather labor intensive, requiring the assistance of acquisitions staff in order to verify current prices. (Approximately 80 percent of the PSU holdings have no price listed in the holdings record; however, items currently received through an acquisitions module automatically include the current price information in the record.) After implementing changes to our loan code policies, it became evident that if we assumed material was lost and quickly assessed fines and fees within six weeks of the item becoming overdue, the item quickly came back with as few as four mailed notices! In addition, by billing the exact cost of the edition whenever possible, we greatly curtailed patrons' temptation to try to buy their own replacement copies, which might be dissimilar editions or have different bindings. They were not only assessed the same price they would have to pay at the local bookstore, but also added fines and nonrefundable processing fees.

BLOCKING THE PATRON'S RECORD

With the exception of faculty, all patrons with fines or fees are immediately suspended from additional borrowing privileges until all material is returned and all fines and fees are paid or resolved. Billing more quickly encouraged the return of lost materials, but significant charges in fines and processing fees (a $5 processing fee for each item billed as lost) often were not paid unless, as mentioned above, the patron requested a transcript or attempted to enroll. For these individuals, the registrar's hold is quite effective as long as they actively pursue university services. For those who are community patrons or who withdraw from classes, the debt remains on their patron records for up to a year before they are turned over to the state for setoff procedures.

POSTAGE AND COSTS

As stated above, the Kansas Setoff Program mandates a minimum of three attempts to contact the patron. In mailing reminders or notices, one must also consider the total amount of the fines or fees versus the cost of postage. In some cases, sending notices by registered mail may be of some benefit. In others, particularly for the smaller fines that do not meet the criteria of setoff minimum, it may not pay to mail the notices. For example, if the fine is only $1.00 and you have mailed four notices at 0.32 each, the library gains nothing financially by the payment of the $1.00 fine.

Use of e-mail and more sophisticated electronic notification systems (ENS) give libraries choices on both ends of the cost spectrum. While e-mail notification among faculty, staff, and students may at first seem a relatively low-cost way to save postage fees, it may also be very difficult to document in terms of bounced messages, discontinued e-mail accounts, or verifying receipt of "delivery." If the mailserver was down, does that constitute a valid notification attempt? Sites utilizing much more costly voice-mail systems require hardware, software, phone lines, and, to an extent, individuals to monitor and maintain the system. For high volume libraries these systems can be well worth the investment. But into each of these approaches to notification a little paper and a lot of staff time must fall if we are to document the notification properly for setoff.

OUT OF STATE, OUT OF REACH

In considering the effectiveness of setoff programs one must also consider how many patrons will be affected; that is, how many will fall under the jurisdiction of the agency that is contracted to do the setoff work. In the case of PSU, the garnishment of wages and tax refunds works only if the delinquent patrons are residents of the State of Kansas or have some business with the State of Kansas. We do not have this formal agreement with the State of Missouri, even though one-third of our patrons live in Missouri, five miles away. There are two possible solutions. One is to find a private collection agency for those who do not fall under the jurisdiction of the State of Kansas. The other, going back to Mendelson's initial data on collection theories, is to modify our loan code and tighten application procedures for out-of-state residents. As the mission statement of the library and the university strongly emphasizes our responsibilities to the community at large regardless of the fact that we are sandwiched between several state borders, we have no current recourse for out-of-state debtors other than registrar holds.

It is worth noting, however, what segment of the patron population is actually responsible for what percentage of the debt. Adjustments to setoff procedures and loan code policies can then be made accordingly.

THE SETOFF CONTACT

A simple Uncollectible Account form is turned in at least once a year to the Student Loan Office at PSU, which coordinates the State Setoff Program for PSU and forwards the forms en masse to the state offices in Topeka. The form includes the patron's full name, last known address, social security number, the type of debt (fines, processing fees, lost book), the date of the last transaction, the date of the last contact, and the balance due.

Payments to the library are made as the Setoff process occurs throughout the year. PSU is assessed the collection fees, and the full amount of the patron's debt is credited to the patron record as the Setoff money is received. In some instances, where a person may only have a $30 income tax refund but the fines may be $200, the $30 refund is credited to the patron's Setoff balance, and the patron's balance of $170 remains in place for the possibility of next year's garnishment.

In addition, should patrons choose the route of appeal, conference calls or travel to Topeka are in store for a representative of the library. In cases of appeal, faxes of all pertinent documents and paperwork concerning the patron need to be delivered to the Setoff office and re-sent to the patron initiating the appeal. The first such appeal that I participated in was a conference call disputing a pre-automation fine from the early 1980s, back when check-out cards were still signed and stapled to the metal clipped overdue card. Oddly enough, it was rather satisfying to fax a copy of the check-out card with the patron's signature on it, which matched exactly the patron's signature on the written appeal form saying he did not remember checking out the material.

ELECTRONIC VERSUS PAPER

Instances such as the one cited above from the good old days of paper check-out cards in the backs of the books, coupled with typed carbon pack reminder forms that served as overdue notices, are archaic reminders of our past. These relics provided tangible evidence that often is not recorded in any manner in the electronic age of automated systems. Dates from postmarks on returned envelopes or dates that forwarding envelopes were received back were very useful as paper evidence.

Collecting and maintaining accurate data should be the foremost concern for librarians, as Mendelson pointed out earlier. We must have in place sufficient safeguards, redundancy checks, software reliability testing, and personal confidence in our practices and procedures leading up to the day when the patron's debt is actually set off. In some cases, the potential for the electronic evidence going "poof" before our very eyes is rather alarming. Even in an age of debit and credit cards, errors do happen. Automation is almost too easy; it is a lot harder to forge a patron's signature than it is to accidentally delete an electronic fine from a patron's record.

When errors do occur, often one needs to scrutinize both the paper and electronic paths to track down the source of those errors.

BACKING UP THE DATA

Unintentional human and machine error complicates the process. Disk drives go bad, usually on weekends. Particularly in the early years of library automation, data processing personnel often lacked sensitivity to the types of information recorded on our automated systems. Understanding how library data was gathered turned into a learning experience for both library and computing center alike.

In early efforts of automation, trying to keep transactions as confidential as possible we avoided running excess printouts, which used up valuable natural resources and potentially revealed who had checked out what. One of my first experiences with a computing center director occurred on a homegrown circulation system, when we discovered the system had had massive disk failure and we lost three days of transactions over one weekend. When the system came back up with new disks, the library was instructed to "re-enter your check-out transactions" and all would be well. From what? Dead silence. This was not payroll data where we could call the local bank and ask, "How much did we deposit on Friday afternoon?" We had no way of knowing which patrons had which books, and we did not have a single scrap of paper backup of any transaction to work backward from. The very next day a printer was installed to capture transactions in a screen-print mode, and the printout was stored religiously every day in a filing cabinet until it was time for shredding and recycling at the end of each semester. Twice more, over a period of three years, this printout saved the day.

ASSIGNMENT OF THE ID

Another suspicious variable in library services is the concept of the unique ID. I say "concept" because I do not believe there is a single library with supposedly flawless plans to assign barcodes or other unique ID numbers to patrons that has not ended up with duplicate

IDs. Our first 150 numbers in a test of a new campus photo ID were all duplicated, simply because as a result of a programming error the first file of 150 people was never saved to disk. "Oh yeah, we can fix that," said the programmer. In the meanwhile, the first 150 patrons to receive their IDs began accruing fines, while the second 150 patrons to receive IDs got "recycled" barcode numbers. Another stellar day in the life of the circulation librarian!

VERIFICATION OF SOFTWARE PROGRAMS

As a site that frequently beta tests software for a major automation vendor, we often have periods where a new code does strange things. While we take responsibility and offer a lot of "grace" to our patrons during these periods, software bugs do occur. (Although I might add that the tendency of the software is usually to make the fines disappear, good news for our patrons!) In the situation of the duplicate IDs, we were fortunate to have a paper record of fines and were able not only to identify the problem, but to resolve it very quickly. Sites that had no paper redundancy simply lost revenue and were unaware of the problem. Grace, in these cases, should always be liberally applied.

INVENTORY AND SCOPE

In most cases, the amount of fines or fees assessed for legitimately checked out material pales in comparison to value of items stolen, damaged, or hidden in our stacks. When a patron claims to have returned an item, what percentage of the items do we find in our libraries? Is a 10 percent error rate acceptable? Five percent? Two percent? What percentage of our transactions billed as lost or late are due to staff problems, disruption in workflow patterns, misshelving, or inventory control issues?

These are all considerations that need to be evaluated and monitored regularly within the library to ensure accurate setoff billing. If the collection is only inventoried once every ten years, and we find even half-a-dozen valid items claimed returned ten years later, are we not causing substantial angst to patrons who may be depending on an income tax refund for payment of critical debts in their own lives?

UNDERSTANDING EQUALS ACCURACY

Especially when using automated systems, understanding what the system is analyzing or reporting is critical to the accuracy of the setoff data. Training our staff to notice when fines are assessed incorrectly, when a system calendar may not be updating properly, or when printed overdue notices are missing information—these are all vital in giving credibility to our setoff programs. Our staff and student workers need to be proactive in understanding the processes and the procedures of both the institution and the computer system. We need to get beyond fining patrons just because "the computer says so"; our training and understanding of the processes must ensure that the data is correct and accurate.

ELECTRONIC DATA COLLECTION PROCEDURES

For the moment, let us assume that our stacks are in order, our software is working correctly, our bar-code scanners are working properly, and all IDs have been assigned to patrons with security that would make the Pentagon proud. We assume that all variables inside the library are functioning at peak efficiency and with a minimum of human error. We have made every effort to give the patron the benefit of the doubt by checking the shelves, and we either have fines due or simply do not have the book in hand—so the setoff process begins.

In the example presented earlier, the setoff data is comprised of name, last known address, social security number, type of debt (fines, lost material, processing fees), balance due, date of last transaction, and date of last contact. Forwarding this information to the state in an electronic format would also appear to be fairly simple: extracting seven fields of data, sending them electronically by flagging the appropriate electronic records, and transmitting them to Topeka.

INTERWOVEN REDUNDANCY

PSU uses at least four component-redundancy strategies to ensure that steps along the payment process are done correctly. These involve separate data files, paper files, and even distinctly separate computer systems with unique log-ins and access. Redundancy can always be overdone, but as explained below, it can also be effective.

First, data is recorded in the patron's personal and confidential record either by manually entering information from a standard application form or by receiving an existing computer record of student information. This information generally includes name, full address, city/state/zip, phone, social security number, and driver's license number if the patron is over sixteen years of age.

The second component of patron-record information is the transaction file, where bar codes of the bibliographic items provide the link between patron and transactions. This file contains check-out and due dates, unresolved fines and fees, dates and times of notice printing, partial payments, staff notes, and any other pertinent transactions.

The third component of the patron data is the corresponding paper "fines card" that PSU continues to maintain as an abbreviated backup of the data on the transaction record. The paper record serves two purposes. One is writing notes on the back of it, such as, "Joe Patron called in today and said his girlfriend would come in and pay this as of March 1—sj 2/24/96." While the annotation may be in cryptic handwriting, it indicates phone or personal contact, who said what when, and gives the library information that may determine the last contact or intent of the patron, which is particularly valuable in cases of appeal. The second purpose of paper record is to note local appeals and other actions by the library staff or patron in attempting to resolve fines, such as stacks searches, patron's claimed time and date of return, or location of return (bookdrop, other site, handed to a person inside, etc.).

If no fines card is found, but the computer transactions have not been cleared to a balance of zero, library staff leap into "supersleuth" mode, ensuring that our paper audit path matches our computer records. If a disparity occurs, it may mean that a cash payment for a fine has been taken and the computer record not reconciled. It may reflect a new-student training issue, or something as simple as a student not knowing how to alphabetize cards. It may also be a patron's name change.

The fourth set of data resides in the registrar's computer. If a fines card and transaction screen both exist, the patron's debt is then crosslisted with the registrar's hold system. This allows us to place transcript holds on all patrons, whether they are enrolled or not. (This also blocks potential students from enrolling until their fines are paid. These are usually community patrons or high school students who have used the library before enrolling in classes at PSU.) This registrar's record is used by all administrative offices on the campus, including Admissions, Student Loan, Registrar, and Parking. Later, when the setoff payment is collected, the registrar's system allows correct real-location of the payment to the departments involved in the setoff process: e.g., $34.95 to the library, $20 to the parking division, $300 to residence housing to pay a damage deposit.

Are four levels of data redundancy necessary? Is it worth the time and energy? PSU has found that from time to time our safety nets have been helpful. Are two computer systems necessary? Only if you occasionally have student workers who take no money, tear up cards, and pay the amount on the computer for their friends, thinking no one will notice. . . .

When all of these records are in order and if the fine is at least one year old and is $25 or more, the patron information is then ready for "setoff." Pertinent data elements are collected in a report and transferred to the Uncollectible Accounts worksheet, which is then turned over to the Student Loan Office.

DATA CLEANUP

The axiom "garbage in, garbage out" is true for setoff fines. Even with "idiotproof" interfaces built into the data fields to force standardization of data input, an amazing number of anomalies occur. Periodically the data is checked to see how many variations of the city/state/zip Pittsburg KS 66762 the student workers in the library can create. The next favorite is to see how many of us are creatures of habit, as evidenced by the plethora of entries for Joplin MO 66762 instead of Joplin MO 64801. If the notice was sent to Joplin MO 66762 and it is the library's error, what happens to the notice? Is this a viable contact? Do we send it again? Do we know the address is really Joplin, or does the patron really live in Pittsburg and someone just had Joplin "on the brain" that day with a full moon shining in the window? Similar anomalies occur with phone numbers and driver's licenses. Some are attributed to the patron turning in an updated phone number but not the new address, or moving from state to state but still receiving phone calls at a friend's house or another contact point. This is often a campus data problem, where the local street address reflects a dorm, but the city/state/zip have not been updated and still refer us to Taipei, Taiwan, or some other exotic locale that I'd be delighted to use when mailing off an overdue notice!

STANDARDS IN LIBRARY AUTOMATION

Two NISO standards in a proposed status describe the components of the patron information record (Z39.69-199x) and the transactions record (Z39.70-199x). Neither are fully approved standards as of February 1998, but significant work has been done on them. Their respective elements describe the content of both patron and transaction record structures and give insight into problems and discrepancies in collecting needed data for setoff purposes.

Z39.69: PATRON RECORD DATA ELEMENTS

Starting first with Z39.69, the patron record data elements, one immediately sees that the standard allows for repetitive fields to enter multiple addresses. There are also fields for "date address becomes valid" and "date address becomes invalid," giving information needed to ascertain the precise address to which an overdue notice was mailed at any given time. However, no date/time stamp for these fields is provided, only a "record-level" date/time stamp that records when any part of the patron record was updated. Which element in the record, which field of data? Was a zip code changed, was an address modified, or was a patron status modified?

In this respect, the electronic version of the patron record still falls short of our paper carbon copies and "address return requested" envelopes from the post office. We have no clear way to document which notice went to what address at any given time. A notice marked "address return requested" may be returned to the library and the computer record updated, but that does not show where the second notice was sent if the library mailed the old notice to the new address.

Not knowing who has updated a record and which field was modified is compounded in sites where automatic patron "loads" are done by matching records against registrar or school district data bases. Was the record modified by a person changing a zip code, or was the record modified by a patron load at 3 a.m. in the morning showing new data coming from, say, the alumni office or from school district new-enrollment rosters? And, a suspicion that many of us have, how many times is a more recent address entered by the library overwritten by an outdated address coming from another office that might be behind on paperwork?

It will be interesting to hear the experiences of libraries as the use of ENS and e-mail systems becomes more prevalent. There seems to be a fine art of tracking e-mail address changes alone; how will we attempt to track whether notification has in fact been delivered, and to what address? Does proof of delivery have to be registered mail, or can we create electronic equivalents? The ability to demonstrate consistent and documented notification procedures is a critical component of Mendelson's criteria.

It should also be noted that automated acquisitions systems, which deal in expenditures and tracking of accounts payable, now have much more sophisticated audit paths. Some still only use notes fields, but others combine security log-ins, date/time stamps, and function/amount records with each transaction. This same sort of date/time audit for each required element of a patron record is long "overdue" (pardon the pun).

Z39.70: CIRCULATION TRANSACTIONS STANDARD

Looking at Z39.70-199x, the Circulation Transactions Standard, a fines/fees audit trail is noticeably missing. Other than the due date of the item, any reference to monetary audits is skeletal at best, with the only reference being fields for amount, balance, currency code, and fee type.

Unless we must make duplicate copies of every overdue notice that potentially could be eligible for setoff, transaction records in the system should include date/time each item was due; date/time each item was returned; date/time each notice was generated; date/time of billing notice; amount due for each notice as well as the total balance due at the time each notice, amount waived or partially paid with date and time; rate at which the fine is assessed (loan code fines and rates change over time); type of loan (hourly, rental, weekly, daily); type of material (reference, general circulating, periodical, video) with its associated link to the bibliographic item; overpayment with date and time; refund with date and time, etc. All of these also need to be tracked by port, log-in ID, even additional password or authorization.

The above transaction data becomes even more critical when sites share databases, as do multi-type library consortia. In consortium settings, fines, fees, and variations in loan codes for sites sharing the automated system may (or may not) be reflected in the transaction data. Therefore, all of the transactions listed above need to be further identified by branch, site, or agency. As the trend toward shared resources continues, the data must clearly reflect the different consortium-members' policies, for example: that a loan-rate other than your own was used in assessing the fine because the material was owned by another site, that the fine was paid at a branch other than the branch from which the item was obtained, or that a particular copy of a book may be billed for at a particular site by a default price rather than an exact BIP+ price (price listed in *Books in Print* plus administrative costs). Consortium policies tend to be driven by statistics, and having automated transaction data to strongly support the intra-agency statistics is critical to the success of any automated system in a multi-site consortium.

Significantly larger capacities for notes, comments, appeals, and other staff processes such as stack searching need to be addressed. A single notes field or a supervisory comment field is only of value if it can reflect the date and time of the entry and who is entering the annotation, removing the annotation, or overriding the transaction.

STATISTICS AND BEYOND

Significantly improved reporting capabilities among library automation vendors to output debt printouts would be most helpful. The bottom line on a report summary of how much debt accrues over an administrative fiscal year is enlightening but inevitably leads to more questions: Who has what item? What percentage of borrowers are students? What percentage of money due is for lost items versus fines? What percentage of the borrowers have moved out of the city this year? Which ones should be writeoffs instead of setoffs? [input your director's favorite tag request here], etc.

Other questions often asked about setoff payments include, "After payment, what were the results? How long did it take to get payment back? Is it worth using this setoff agency? What percentage of fines were for books vs. reference material? What percentage of people have paid, what patron class were they from? This is of course made even more difficult by vendors who put paid fines in separate data files from the unpaid fines rather than simply flagging one entry as "paid" or "unpaid" and using the one file.

In some systems, when a fine is paid, the date and time data are nulled out by the system, making historical statistical collection by date and time impossible since the data no longer exist. While breaking the link and clearing the patron record of confidential charges, the loss of data often compromises the ability to evaluate the process and the policies. In other cases, there are customers who are delighted to have "any" automated billing process at all, for whom any statistical or historical analysis is unimportant compared to the drudgery of assessing fines manually. The ability to track partial payments and payments made in different forms (cash, student swipe card, check, credit card)—this, too, needs a much more detailed audit path than most library automation vendors are capable of providing at this time.

FUTURE OF SETOFF PROCEDURES

The bottom line for most libraries with automated systems is that we need to review carefully what our systems are reporting. Libraries need to build in local procedures and, if necessary, paper trails to ensure that the data used in evaluating setoff processes is accurate, consistent, and carefully and correctly documented. Most automated systems that have been on the market for any length of time were designed with circulation as a first core module in the 1980s. Very few vendors have made significant changes or enhancements in their circulation modules to reflect more sophisticated gathering of statistics or electronic output of data for projects such as setoff. Nor have they provided tools or utilities to manage automated data pertaining to patrons and fines more effectively.

In the future, we may be able to store a photo image of the patron right in the patron record, or perhaps a photo image of the complete driver's license and the patron's signature, or any other ID accepted at the time of checkout. We need to continue to improve the validity and verification necessary in all patron data, including which library personnel have permission to update or modify each data field and a date and time stamp for each field.

We need to protect our patrons' confidentiality. However, we must also continue to improve information available to us, such as the fine structure at the time of assessment or bibliographic information. Many of us still have the luxury of using the same fine structure that was in place when we brought up our automated systems; this will eventually change, and we will need to understand the old fines and their rates. Bibliographic records may be withdrawn, discarded, or otherwise obliterated to ensure more accurate holdings in our online catalogs, but the circulation staff will still have a need to identify the bibliographic elements removed, including cost, edition, and call number, should any of the charges be appealed or the information needed for setoff verification.

Transactional data need to be clearly stated unambiguously on the staff terminals and screens. The data must also be able to withstand transfer from one automated system to another without losing patron, transaction, or bibliographic integrity. Input quality must be accurate and supported by good interfaces. Our understanding of the data, the process, and the procedures continue to be the best defenses for all our patrons to ensure an effective setoff effort.

ACKNOWLEDGMENTS

Thanks to Bob Walter, Bill Draper, Mary Wolfe, and John Weible for their assistance in making the "process" work!

REFERENCES

Bremer, Galen. Personal communication. February-March 1996.

Mendelson, Roger. "A Simple Guide to Solving Your Book Return Problem." *Australian Library Journal* (August 1994) 155–157.

National Information Standards Organization. NISO Z39.70-199X, Proposed American National Standard Format for Circulation Transactions Standard. 1993. NISO Press, Oxon Hill, MD.

National Information Standards Organization. NISO Z39.69-199X, Proposed American National Standard for Patron Record Data Elements. 1992. NISO Press, Oxon Hill, MD.

State of Kansas. Department of Administration, Division of Accounts and Reports. *Using the Setoff Program to Collect Accounts Receivable*. October 11, 1995.

Kansas Statutes, 75 KSA 6201. Setoff against debtors of the state, municipalities and certain foreign states.

Kansas Statutes, 785 KSA 6205. Setoff against debtors of the state, municipalities and certain foreign states (minimum debt setoff; maximum setoff against earnings).

PART III:
MORE ABOUT
MANAGING OVERDUES

8 LIBRARY FINES RECONSIDERED: THE PHILOSOPHY OF CHARGING FINES

by Julie Walker

ATHENS REGIONAL LIBRARY SYSTEM
ATHENS, GEORGIA

In the sixteen years since Patsy Hansel and Robert Burgin did their landmark study of library overdues (see Preface), there has been no systematic analysis of the effectiveness of overdue fines in retrieving materials in a timely fashion. Hansel and Burgin, in their oft-quoted North Carolina study, found that "there were no significant differences in the overdues rates between libraries that charge fines and those that do not."[1] However, the authors did note a tendency in libraries that do not charge fines to get their books back more slowly, "but they ultimately get more of them back."[2] In other words, charging fines does not significantly improve a library's ability to encourage the prompt return of materials, but libraries with no fines actually may expect to have lower overall loss rates of materials. Depending upon the primary goal of the library, these findings could be used to argue for or against a fines policy.

Much has changed in the world of public libraries in recent years. Automation has revolutionized the way circulation functions are handled, and in no area more than the management of overdue materials. In fact, more efficient and accurate record-keeping, leading to more careful management of library resources, is a key rationale for implementation of automated circulation systems. Automation has removed some of the arguments libraries have used for eliminating overdue fines. The amount of clerical time required to manage fines and the accounting process was vast before the widespread use of computers. Today's automated systems almost invisibly calculate amounts owed, amounts paid, and send notices at the touch of a key.

Clearly, the decision to charge fines is not an issue to be resolved only with hard numbers. Instead, libraries across America have used a variety of rationales to determine and justify their fine policies. Issues as diverse as public relations and patrons' reactions, inescapable financial concerns, deeply-held opinions of library staff and administration, and the moral imperative of fines to teach a much-needed lesson have been used to support fines. Conversely, the compassionate view of our higher purpose of free public library service to all has been cited as a determining factor in not charging fines. Below, in interviews with public librarians from libraries large and small, we explore an issue which still has no clear answers.

PUBLIC RELATIONS

It would seem that the public relations advantage of not charging fines would be undisputed; however, librarians do disagree on the PR value of a no-fines policy. Janie Hill, of the Marrowbone Public Library District in Bethany, Illinois, finds that "the public loves not having fines, and it is great PR. It is not well-received from our neighbor libraries. There is a great deal of reciprocal borrowing in our rural area, and they don't like to hear "But Bethany doesn't charge fines!"[3] A Massachusetts library director who is currently experimenting with a fine-free year concurs. "The patrons are delighted. We have a 'conscience jar' on the desk so that those who feel particularly guilty can contribute to the Friends of the Library . . . From the end of June through the end of October we turned $181.97 over to the Friends."[4] "Having no fines does not eliminate (or in our case, substantially reduce) confrontations with patrons across the charge desk," reports Harry J. Dutcher, director of the Saratoga Springs (N.Y.) Public Library. "It seems as though patrons are inclined to keep 'no fines' items out longer; although, if they care about their borrowing privileges, they eventually come back. This results in bills for long overdue books, overdues that prevent further borrowing, etc. In our experience, the public relations advantage librarians speak of hasn't been there."[5]

IF NOT FINES . . .

Dutcher's comments remind us that fines are not the only "stick" we have in encouraging patrons to return materials in a timely fashion. Many libraries have stringent rules rescinding borrowing privileges for patrons with overdue materials. Sally Armstrong, head of circulation at Santa Fe (New Mexico) Public Library, describes her library's approach: "Several years ago, we set up the rule of three. If you have three or more items overdue, or *any* item overdue more than three months, you cannot check out any more things until you clear up your record (return or pay) . . . So you can see, we are not total cream puffs."[6] The Somerville (New Jersey) Free Public Library, experimenting with a fine-free year, saw an alarming increase in overdue materials until an aggressive overdue-notice campaign was begun. "When a book was two weeks overdue, the patron was sent a notice and placed on the blacklist. This meant that until the patrons returned their overdue books, they could not take out more books. If, after two more weeks, the books still were not back, the patrons received a second notice billing them for the items . . . For most of the library's patrons . . . , this "no-lend" policy worked effectively."[7]

IT ALL COMES DOWN TO MONEY

"It has been my observation that libraries which do *not* charge fines are absolutely sold on the issue. Whereas libraries that do seem to always be thinking about *not* doing it!"[8] noted Dusty Gres, director of the Ohoopee Regional Library System in Vidalia, Georgia. Many library administrators, however, feel that they have little choice in the matter as they rely on the income produced by fines for essential funding. "In our very tight budget schemes, fines are the only way we can pay the part-time college and high school students. Income from fines for these hourly workers made up about 6 percent of this year's budget. That's quite a significant amount"[9] commented Kathryn Ames, director of the Athens Regional Library System in Athens, Georgia. Libraries that do not themselves receive the fine monies are often more willing to consider eliminating fines. Sally Armstrong of Santa Fe Public Library, where fines collected went into the city's general fund, noted, "I know that in a way we eventually benefit from the money we collect, since we are funded out of that same general fund, but it doesn't *feel* as if we do. If the money could go right into our own line item for the book budget, we might have a different attitude."[10] The significant majority of librarians interviewed who currently charge fines cite the need for the income as their primary reason for not considering eliminating fines. Likewise, most libraries that do not charge fines, like Santa Fe and Forsyth County, North Carolina, would not directly receive any monies collected and, therefore, feel less of a loss of revenue from a no-fines policy. Sherri L. Lazenby, director of the San Benito (Tex.) Public Library, comments "At all of the libraries I have worked, the libraries don't get the fine money for overdue books; the city governments do. I personally don't care if I ever collect a fine as long as I get the book back."[11]

Other librarians view the cost of charging fines in a different light. "There are instances where charging fines can be more expensive than any revenue to be derived," asserts Oak Lawn (Illinois) Public Library Director James Casey. "I often tell patrons that the library doesn't even recover costs in dealing with overdues. Staff time is the single most expensive component of any library budget. Irate patrons often complain at the desk, to the unit head, department head and up to the director. You must listen respectfully to taxpayers, but it all costs time and money."[12]

HOW MUCH TO FINE?

Debbie Manget, director of the Conyers-Rockdale Library in Conyers, Georgia, notes, "We have the highest overdue book fine in the state: $.20 per day. The Board doubled it a couple of years ago . . . We were surprised that we received very few complaints or comments when the increase occurred. We do believe that it helps us get our materials back quicker (from conversations with patrons)."[13] Harry Dutcher of Saratoga Springs believes, "If you have fines, make them meaningful. I'm convinced that one of the worst things librarians do is the 'you owe us a dime' syndrome. It makes us look like silly, fussy bureaucrats fretting over nothing. I would suggest forgiving all fines under $.50 or $1.00, but making the maximum for most items fairly steep—we go to $10.00 per item at $.10 per day. These two policies keep us from hassling the responsible patron who is slightly late with an item and provides a real deterrent (or eliminates) the patron whom I would describe as having crossed the line from 'I borrowed it' to 'I stole it.'"[14]

"I HATE FINES"

Karen Hicklin, director of the Livingston County Library in Chillicothe, Missouri, belongs to the "I hate fines" school of thought. She says, "When we moved to an automated system, we were having to rethink everything, including fines. I hated them, my staff hated them, and very likely the public hated them." Her library eliminated fines on August 1, 1994, after deciding "we really didn't have much to lose." According to Hicklin's calculations, her former fine revenue roughly equalled her costs of retrieving overdues. By allowing the new, automated system to mail one notice, her new system costs were one-half as much as the old. Hicklin cites "the positive response from the public and the relief of the staff that they are no longer required to police that particular aspect of our business" as the best results of the decision to eliminate fines.[15] "I do not believe in fines," asserts Sally Armstrong, head of circulation at Santa Fe Public Library. "In fact, I have set it up so people can bring me some other book (only if they arrange it first) to replace the lost one. And if they are having a financial squeeze, I will let them work off the cost of the book by shelving. We figure how much they owe, divide it by the $6/hour we pay shelvers, and set them to work."[16]

TEACHING A LESSON

Despite the observation that "the levying of fines, like any punitive approach to overdues, diverts attention from the basic cultural, educational, informational, and recreational goals of the library"[17], many librarians today still speak in terms of punishing offenders when queried about fines. Library fines are tradition. The threat of a fine provides the patron with an incentive for returning materials on time, a penalty for returning materials late, and an education in being a responsible citizen. It is claimed that fines represent a correct posture for librarians to take in response to the generally irresponsible character of our society.[18] Front-line circulation staff, who deal daily with the problems of overdue materials, are often the strongest advocates of this point of view. "I gave in to pressure from my clerical staff to charge a fine when an overdue notice had been sent. After handling so many overdues, the clerks became irritated that there was no 'pay-off,' so to speak,"[19] reports Gerry Baldwin, director of the Desmond-Fish Library in Garrison, New York. Dusty Gres, of Vidalia, Georgia, says, "The older I get, the more I wrestle with this issue, and the more I see the library and the taxpayers abused—the more I believe in fines and penalties."[20] Often it is the library's board of trustees who wish to see the punishment of overdue fines administered. Karen Hicklin of Chillicothe reports "The board was skeptical [about eliminating fines]. We had lots of discussion about how kids could afford to buy candy bars but always seemed to have empty pockets when it came to paying fines."[21]

Do fines, with their connotation of punishment and regulation, run contrary to the image we truly wish to convey—one of an institution that is free, open to all, flexible, concerned for the community? Harry J. Dutcher points out, "I am often amazed by the fact that librarians who take on censorship issues with great zeal show little or no concern about the many, many patrons denied library service because of relatively small fine records. We'll go to the wall for the right to borrow one controversial title but show little or no concern when a child goes through twelve years of school unable to use the library because his parents brought him to the library, borrowed a $15 picture book, and never returned it."[22]

"COUNTER TO THE SPIRIT OF THE LIBRARY BILL OF RIGHTS"

Those who would argue against charging fines often point out that fines may well negate our many efforts to draw people into our libraries, to present a welcoming image with few barriers, and to serve those without the means to pay for services. "We developed a way of explaining our unusual policy that talked about the fact that fines ended up penalizing the very people we should be encouraging to use the library . . . especially children, the elderly, and people of limited means,"[23] explains Sally Armstrong. In 1990 the Public Library of Youngstown (Ohio) and Mahoning County implemented a no-fine policy for juvenile materials "to eliminate a possible barrier to library use by children," according to Library Director Theresa Trucksis. "Sometimes a child is reprimanded by a parent for not returning books on time and after paying a fine told not to use the library any more."[24] The Library staff and trustees hoped to eliminate the monetary obstacle to library use by adopting the no-fines policy on a trial basis.

RESULTS IN THE REAL WORLD

The results, however, for Youngstown and Mahoning County were less than satisfactory. Raffaella Pazak, director of Branches and Children's Services, reports that fines for juvenile materials were reinstituted after one year. "The books weren't coming back," Pazak reports. "We thought fines were an obstacle for our patrons, but we found just the opposite. The policy was impacting what we had available for circulation, and our regular patrons were complaining. It just didn't work for us."[25] In this case, an effort to extend services without barriers created an unforeseen problem of actually denying access to materials.

At the Livingston County Library, eliminating fines generated positive results for circulation and return rates. Karen Hicklin reports circulation numbers that show a remarkable outcome of their fine-free experiment: "Comparing the first seven months of 1994 with the same period in 1995, our circulation has increased 12.75 percent, the number of people contacted for overdues has decreased by 68 percent, and the number of items overdue has been reduced by 90 percent. We were hoping for good things when we stopped fining people, but we are stunned at this change."[26]

January Adams, reference librarian at Somerville Free Public Library, reported mixed results from their fine-free trial in 1990. Since the library had been implementing a number of changes in operations and ambiance, the library staff felt they could not attribute increases in circulation only to the elimination of fines. However, "staff realized with pleasure that life at the circulation desk was definitely much easier. Those working at the desk no longer had to calculate fines, take payments, and make change. Patrons and staff had become less defensive about overdue books and a few patrons even joked about being put on the dreaded blacklist."[27] Adams noted that the library's goal of increasing the return of very late materials was not achieved. In fact, the percentage of total circulation overdue and items never returned actually increased very slightly during the fine-free year.[28]

At the end of 1990, Somerville decided to extend the no-fine policy indefinitely. "The library decided that the loss of revenue from the elimination of overdue-book fines does not outweigh the library's desire to build a more positive, less threatening image."[29] Carolyn Stephani, director of the Somerville Free Public Library confirms the success of Somerville's experimental fine-free year. "This policy works very well for us. The patrons are still amazed, actually, that we don't have fines, but they love it." Although Stephani inherited the fine-free policy when she took over at Somerville in 1994, she agrees that the bookkeeping required by fines was simply not worth the payoff, and that eliminating fines "saves an awful lot of hassle."[30]

PHILOSOPHY

In the end, fines are but one aspect of library services and programs, customized and refined to fit every differing community's needs and standards. Hard numbers alone cannot prove or disprove the effectiveness of fines in increasing the timely return of library materials. Each library, with the considerations of financial constraints, community preferences, automated circulation functions, staffing, and library board and library directors' philosophies, must determine whether fines are an effective tool, furthering the mission of the library, or an unnecessary burden to staff and patrons alike.

REFERENCES

1. Hansel, Patsy and Robert Burgin. "Hard Facts About Overdues." *Library Journal* 108 (February 15, 1983) 350.
2. Ibid, 350.
3. Janie Hill, personal interview, 17 November 1995
4. Marnie Oakes, personal interview, 9 December 1995
5. Harry J. Dutcher, letter to the author, 15 November 1995
6. Sally Armstrong, personal interview, 6 December 1995
7. Adams, January. "A Year of Living Dangerously: Implementation of a No-Fines Policy at Somerville Free Public Library." *Public Libraries* 30 (November-December 1991) 347.
8. Dusty Gres, personal interview, 15 January 1996
9. Kathryn Ames, personal interview, 5 December 1995
10. Armstrong, interview.
11. Sherri L. Lazenby, letter to Publib discussion list, 29 December 1995.
12. James B. Casey, personal interview, 28 November 1995
13. Deborah Manget, letter to the author, 12 January 1996
14. Dutcher, letter to author.
15. Karen Hicklin, personal interview, 14 January 1996
16. Armstrong, interview.
17. Anderson, Barbara. "Overdues and the Library's Image," in *Library Overdues*, ed. Patsy Hansel and Robert Burgin (New York: Haworth, 1984), 115.
18. Anderson, Barbara. "The Fines-No Fines Debate," in *Library Overdues*, ed. Patsy Hansel and Robert Burgin, 106.
19. Gerry Baldwin, letter to the author, 16 November 1995.
20. Gres, interview.
21. Hicklin, interview.
22. Dutcher, letter to the author.
23. Armstrong, interview.
24. "Upfront News." *Wilson Library Bulletin* 64 (June 1990) 13.
25. Raffaella Pazak, personal interview, 26 January 1996.
26. Karen Hicklin, letter to Publib discussion list, 20 October 1995.
27. Adams, 347.
28. Ibid., 347
29. Ibid., 349
30. Carolyn Stephani, personal interview, 26 January 1996.

9 OVERDUES: A SELECT BIBLIOGRAPHY
by Terry B. Prather

TO FINE OR NOT TO FINE

Adams, January. "A Year of Living Dangerously: Implementation of a No-Fine Policy at Somerville Free Public Library." *Public Libraries* 30 (November/December 1991): 346–9.

The Somerville (New Jersey) Public Library eliminated overdue-book fines for a trial period. Although the results were not quite what had been hoped for, it was determined that the beneficial aspects of the policy outweighed the negative elements, and the plan was extended indefinitely.

Anderson, A. J. et al. "You Must Teach Kids Responsibility." *Library Journal* 109 (May 1, 1984): 867–9.

This "How Do You Manage?" case study presents a librarian, new on the job, who challenges and does not enforce the library's policy of denying children and young adults borrowing privileges if they owe the library money. Three librarians present scenarios for how the supervisor should handle the situation.

Anderson, Barbara L. "The Fines—No Fines Debate." *Library and Archival Security* 6, no. 2/3 (summer/fall 1984): 105–11.

Advocates of fines for overdue materials see fines as an incentive for returning materials on time, a display of the library's seriousness about its rules, and as a generator of income. On the other side, those advocating the elimination of fines argue that fines do not make a significant difference in a library's overdues, they are a hardship on children, they cost more to adminster than they bring in, and they damage the library's image. The debate continues.

"Dallas Public Gets Tough on Overdues." *Wilson Library Bulletin* 59 (September 1984): 14.

In a campaign called "Get the Books Back," this library assessed fines of up to $50 per day for overdue materials. The second phase of the campaign consisted of arrest warrants for people who did not respond to repeated warnings.

Greiner, J. M. "Professional Views: The Philosophy and Practice of Fines and Fees." *Public Libraries* 28 (September/October 1989): 256–61.

The views of members representing each of the Public Library Association sections show different philosophies as well as common threads of concern for the user and the library.

Handy, A. E. "Librarian's True Confessions: I Stopped Doing Overdues—for Three Years!" *Book Report* 10 (November/December 1991): 37–8.

The author tells about the adventure of stopping overdues and the disadvantages of doing so in this "true confession."

Kaur, Amarjit. "Overdue Charges for Overdue Books. A Literature Survey from 1975 to 1985." *Herald of Library Science* 25 (July/October 1986): 200–3.

A brief overview of the literature on overdues for the decade 1975–85.

"Mahoning Tries No-Fine Policy." *Wilson Library Bulletin* 64 (June 1990): 13.

The Public Library of Youngstown (Ohio) and Mahoning County tried a trial period of no fines to see if it would encourage children to use the library.

"Massachusetts Gets Tough on Overdues." *Wilson Library Bulletin* 65 (November 1990): 12.

The state of Massachusetts passed a new law that defined larceny of library property and willful failure to return library materials as crimes. Fines for larceny were as high as $25,000 and imprisonment, for overdue materials up to $500.

"Milwaukee Gets Tough on Overdue Books." *Wilson Library Bulletin* 62 (April 1988): 13.

To save postage and encourage borrowers to return materials promptly, the Milwaukee (Wisconsin) Federated Library System decided to issue only one overdue notice. Borrowers who do not return materials within two weeks of the notice will lose their borrowing privileges.

"Milwaukee Public Library Cancels Fines for Children." *School Library Journal* 38 (June 1992): 16.

The Milwaukee (Wisconsin) Public Library stopped charging fines for children and forgave all past fines in an attempt to get children to use their library cards.

"Minneapolis Raises Overdue Fines." *Wilson Library Bulletin* 65 (March 1991): 11.

The new policy raised the daily fine for overdue library materials from \$.20 to \$.25 per day, up to a maximum of \$7.00.

"No Fines Saves Money for Sidney, Ohio Library." *Library Journal* 110 (March 1, 1985): 28.

The library ventured into a two-year experiment of not charging fines. A recent check shows less than 1 percent of circulating books are now overdue and the processing costs are minimal.

"Stiff Fines in Massachusetts Provoke Annoyance, Public Misperception of a Stronger Overdue/Defacement Statute Creates Unease." *Library Journal* 115 (October 15, 1990): 31.

A new state law that strengthens penalties for overdue materials is being misrepresented. Although the new law has brought back a flood of overdues, it has inspired the local media to exaggerate the public's fear of being tossed into jail for overdues—which in reality is not an option. Also missed and obscured is the \$1.1 million the library loses each year in unreturned library materials.

OVERDUES AND THE LIBRARY'S IMAGE

Anderson, Barbara L. "Overdues and the Library's Image." *Library and Archival Security* 6, no. 2/3 (summer/fall 1984): 113–21.

The public perceives librarians to be inflexible and rule-oriented; such an image discourages library use. Contributing to the image are rules such as those dealing with overdue materials. The author encourages librarians to ensure that all policies and other details of the library be consistent with attempts to encourage library use.

Baldwin, Michael. "Library Fines: The Semantic Solution." *Public Libraries* 29 (March/April 1990): 99–100.

Has the long-standing practice of charging overdues adversely affected our relationship with our clientele by causing us to treat them as criminals? Baldwin proposes that this negative connotation be corrected by converting the "fines" concept to one of paid privilege.

Caywood, Carolyn. "Penny Wise, Pound Foolish." *School Library Journal* 40 (November 1994): 44.

Virginia Beach public librarian doubts whether the fines libraries collect are sufficient to pay for the cost of collecting them. And that's only the direct cost; it doesn't take into account the damage done to the library's image as a free institution open to everyone.

Glover, L. A. "The Other Side of the Fence." *Book Report* 10 (May/June 1991): 18–19.

A school librarian begins to question the effects on students that doubting their excuses for overdue books has.

"Minneapolis Library Drops Plan to Raise Children's Fines to Increase Revenue." *School Library Journal* 42 (October 1996): 12–13.

A proposal to raise juvenile fines at the Hennepin County Library was shelved after it sparked opposition from staff members and a negative article in the local press. But library managers plan to revisit the idea, which is part of an effort to find new revenue sources to offset declining property taxes.

Mitchell, W. Bede. "On the Use of Positive Reinforcement to Minimize the Problem of Overdue Library Materials." *Journal of Library Administration* 9, no. 3 (1988): 87–101.

The author discusses the pros and cons of reducing the problem of overdue materials using positive reinforcement as a substitute for, or in addition to, fines. An operant conditioning model is used.

Moxley, Melody. "In Search of Excellence: How One Public Library Copes with Overdues." *Library and Archival Security* 6, no. 1/2 (summer/fall 1984): 19–28.

The article outlines an overdue procedure for a public library that has been able to reduce its overdue rate. The library sends two notices, gives a six-day grace period for circulated materials that are overdue, uses one fine slip, and relies on legal actions for patrons with over $50 in overdue materials. Sample forms are included.

"Questions to Ask ... The Basics: Public Good and Opportunity Costs." *Bottom Line* 3, no. 3 (1989): 5.

The author explains briefly the meaning of public good, economic externality, and opportunity cost. Overdue fines are based on the economic concept of opportunity cost.

AUTOMATION

Bates, Wilma H. "Managing Overdues in the School Library." *Library and Archival Security* 6, no. 2/3 (summer/fall 1984): 83–90.

The article examines the overdues procedures of a high-school library with a microcomputer to assist in the process of maintaining a list of students with overdue materials. The school system's regulations and library policies are outlined.

McClintock, Patrick. "Library Automation and Overdues: A Discussion of Possibilites and Potentialities." *Library and Archival Security* 6, no. 2/3 (summer/fall 1984): 97–104.

The article is intended as a guide for libraries that are concerned about the overdue process and are considering automation.

Nelms, Willie. "The Art of Overdues." *Public Library Quarterly* 9, no. 1 (1989): 13–
_____ and D. Taylor. "Overdues Procedures Using a Microcomputer." *Library and Archival Security* 6, no. 1/2 (summer/fall 1984): 91–96.

The two articles, one by Nelms and one by Nelms and Taylor, relate how the Sheppard Memorial Library, Greenville, North Carolina, has applied microcomputer technology to the problem of overdues. A file of patrons with overdue material is maintained, and the computer produces bills and Rolodex cards for a delinquent-patrons file.

"A New Focus on Overdue Fines: Seattle Doubles Fines, Fort Worth Computerizes, Houston Hires Agency." *Library Journal* 117 (February 1, 1992): 18–19.

Fort Worth has turned the chore of sending overdue notices over to a computerized phone-notification system called the Dewey Dialer. They claim this saves nearly $12,000 annually in postage alone; there are also substantial savings in printing, labor, and transportation. Seattle raised their fines, and Houston uses an agency to collect fines and overdue materials.

Tweedie, S. "'Computerized'" Overdue Notices Using FileMaker Plus and a 512 K-enhanced Macintosh [at Markely Elementary Library], in *Macintoshed Libraries*. Apple Library Users Group: 1988 p. 47.

A library sets up a computerized overdue-notice system using Macintosh equipment and software.

TRICKS OF THE TRADE

Farrington, Jean Walter. "Overdues and Academic Libraries: Matters of Access and Collection Control." *Library and Archival Security* 6, no. 2/3 (summer/fall 1984): 67–76.

How overdues are dealt with in an academic library often depends on which group of borrowers is involved. Students, faculty and staff, and outside borrowers all must be treated differently, and there is the potential for serious problems.

Lutz, J. "Oh, They Never Returned!" *Library Journal* 112 (June 15, 1987): 45–6.

The problems of overdue books in this branch library could no longer wait for the day when a great computer would solve the problem. South Branch (Texas) refined the overdue procedure, and the steps are listed here. The results after the two-year change were good.

Moeller-Pfeiffer, Kathleen. "Novel Approaches to Overdues; or The Ones Who Borrow and the Ones Who Lend." *Library and Archival Security* 6, no. 2/3 (summer/fall 1984): 29–39.

Moeller-Pfeiffer looks at current attempts to deal with overdues. The most familiar method—overdue fines—has continued to produce a great deal of debate. The author examines the use of collection agencies, mailgrams, legal proceedings, and the use of a local dispute settlement center.

Powell, Patty. "Outfoxing Overdues in the Hospital Library." *Library and Archival Security* 6, no. 2/3 (summer/fall 1984): 77–82.

Librarians in the small special library can deal with overdues by knowing their users and being creative in reminding patrons about overdue materials. The main overdue problem seems to be absent-mindedness.

Raven, Debby. "London Invests in Recovery Officers." *Library Association Record* 94 (October 1992): 625.

London libraries find that having a book-recovery officer on staff is an excellent investment.

"What We Are Doing about Overdues." *Unabashed Librarian* 57 (1985): 9–10.

Woodland Libraries offer ways that they have developed for handling overdues.

Wright, F. W. "Detective Sniffs Out Overdue Library Books." *American Libraries* 18 (December 1987): 892.

The library in Maitland, Florida, uses the police department and a detective to deal with patrons who have more than $300 worth of materials checked out for an extended period of time. The library has had good luck in getting books back.

LAW AND LEGAL ACTION

"Bad Borrowers End Up in Court [in Derbyshire and Clwyd]. *Library Association Record* 97 (November 1995): 585.

Library users who abuse the borrowing system will face tough new measures. Two county councils have made decisions to take the worst offenders to court. The councils hope the publicity will encourage other abusers to return borrowed materials.

Bries, Kathy. "Check It Out/Get It Back . . . or Else. *Colorado Libraries* 22 (spring 1996): 22–4.

This paper presented at the fourth Circulation Open Forum in Denver, Colorado, tells how twenty-two neighborhood branches and a central branch handled the "problem customer" using the CARL online system. A typical month is highlighted to show the overdue process, and statistics are included. The Denver City Attorney's Collection Office is called upon when problems arise. Before reaching that point, the circulation staff rely on their skills to maintain customer good will and the computer system.

"Felony Charges Cause Influx of Overdues." *American Libraries* 15 (April 1984): 200.

The Cumberland County (North Carolina) attorney filed criminal charges against fifteen delinquent borrowers and announced the intention of serving warrants to fifteen others. Recovery of materials improved 10 percent after the library sent warnings of criminal action.

Gaughan, Thomas M. "Oscar Nominee-Book Thief Pleads No Contest." *American Libraries* 20 (January 1989): 7–8.

In a plea bargain, screenwriter Jerry Gustav Hasford, a 1988 Academy Award nominee, pleaded no contest to possession of stolen property, about 2,000 books stolen from public libraries in seven cities.

Goetz, Art H. "Dealing with Defaulters." *Library and Archival Security* 6, no. 2/3 (summer/fall 1984): 41–9.

The author discusses the use of small-claims-court for dealing with patrons who have overdue materials. The small-claims-court procedures for the state of Maryland are examined in detail, and the author's success with this method is documented.

Goldberg, Beverly. "No Hard Feelings from Patron Jailed over Overdue." *American Libraries* 26 (November 1995): 990.

A Kenton County (Kentucky) Public Library patron was held for seven hours in the county jail for ignoring a court summons over a seventeen-month-overdue library book. She was subsequently interviewed on CNN and NPR but declined to appear on Montel Williams, Inside Edition, and Hard Copy.

Hansel, Patsy. "Three Libraries and Overdue Law." *Library and Archival Security* 6, no. 2/3 (summer/fall 1984): 57–65.

The author presents three case studies of North Carolina public libraries and their experiences with the legal aspect of overdues. One library's procedure for taking delinquent patrons to court is outlined. In another case, the General Assembly enacted a special law for that county. The last case study gives attention to the county commissioners' enacting a local ordinance governing overdue library materials.

"I Won't Go to Another Library As Long As I Live . . . Though They Were Nice to Me at the Jail." *Unabashed Librarian* 69 (1988): 12.

Patron jailed for overdue books does not want to use library again.

Kniffel, Leonard. "Judge Rules Man Liable for Books Checked Out on Lost Card." *American Libraries* 24 (October 1993): 806.

A district judge in Lawrence, Kansas, ruled that a man was liable for $1,050 worth of books checked out from the public library on his card by someone else and never returned. The library had never taken such action against a user before. The library's collection agency had advised taking him to court.

———."Library Sues Maryland Residents for Overdues Worth $2,468." *American Libraries* 22 (October 1991): 831–2.

Twenty-four users of the Carroll County (Maryland) Public Library were sued in civil court for the return of the library materials or the value of the material plus court costs. The library's procedure is detailed.

———. "Woman Jailed in Georgia for Overdue Books." *American Libraries* 20 (December 1989): 1035.

A woman in Gurinnett County, Georgia, with $149.65 in book fines was arrested, held without bond, and released on her own recognizance the following day, pending arraignment.

Mendelson, Roger. "How to Make Legal Action Effective." *The Australian Library Journal* 44 (November 1995): 237–8.

The author, a practicing solicitor, and a director of Purshka Fast Debt Recovery advises public libraries on a strategy for recovering fines or overdue books from borrowers. Among the steps is emphasizing the terms of the contract the borrower is required to sign to obtain a card.

Murray, Marilyn. "Baltimore County Public Library and the Delinquent Borrower." *Library and Archival Security* 6, no. 2/3 (summer/fall 1984): 51–6.

This article explains how Baltimore County (Maryland) Public Library has employed small-claims-court measures in its overdues procedures. The library attempts to contact patrons who have $40 or more in overdue materials. If the patron cannot be contacted and if the patron does not respond to letters, court action is initiated. The results are documented.

"New Jersey Library Barters for Legal Services." *Wilson Library Bulletin* 59 (December 1984): 250.

Notice of overdue materials valued at $50 or more is sent to the county counsel's office, which issues a letter warning of an impending suit. In exchange for their work, the county counsel's office is entitled to equivalent time on the library's WESTLAW database.

"New Jersey Library Seeks Overdues in Court." *Library Journal* 117 (October 1, 1992): 25–6.

Morris County (New Jersey) Library decided to serve summons to about 3,000 patrons with overdue materials well beyond the lending period if the materials are not returned and the fines paid. Because some of the items are irreplaceable getting the materials back is more important than collecting the money.

Pearson, L. R. "And the Winner Is Not . . . Police Seek Oscar Nominee over Library Cache in Locker." *American Libraries* 19 (May 1988): 333–4, 336.

California Polytechnic State University tried to find screenwriter and Academy Award nominee Jerry Hasford, who had unreturned materials amounting to about $2,000. Although the address, phone, and social security number he had given did not lead anywhere, a photo in the newspaper showed him in a local storage area. With a search warrant, the storage locker was searched, and 9,919 library books from different libraries were retrieved.

"Tough Overdues Law Dies When Error Legalizing Rape Found in Omnibus Crime Bill." *American Libraries* 16 (November 1985): 679.

At the urging of the Missouri Library Association (MLA) a bill making it a felony to keep $150 of library materials more than 60 days past the due date was signed into law. Eight days before it went into effect, it was discovered that through a clerical error one section of the bill repealed the rape law, making rape legal. MLA will resubmit its own bill separately.

"Town Sues 21 Patrons for Overdues." *American Libraries* 22 (September 1991): 701. Since the Prescott Public Library (Arizona) installed a CLSI online catalog, the public has turned against people abusing their library privileges. (The catalog reveals a title's status to the searcher.) The public has been aggressively supportive of the action taken by the library and city attorney to file civil lawsuits.

AMNESTY AND FOOD FOR FINES

"Amnesty for St. Louis Patrons." *Library Journal* 112 (May 1, 1987): 22.

St. Louis (Missouri) Public Library declared an amnesty month and retrieved 4,768 items worth about $85,650.

"Book Amnesty Program Proves Patrons 'Can Due' It." *Library Journal* 114 (January 1, 1989): 19.

"Can Due," a book amnesty program, was held by the Springfield (Massachusetts) City Library. All patrons holding overdue books could return them free of charge as long as they gave a can of food to be distributed to the needy.

Bronson, D. A. "Food for Fines." *Georgia Libraries* 29 (fall 1992): 69.

Chestatee (Georgia) Regional Library patrons pay fines with food for the needy.

"Food for Fines." [reprinted from *Granite State Libraries*, October/November 1986]. In *Alternative Library Literature*, 1986–87. McFarland and Co., 1988: 102.

Library combines efforts to retrieve overdue library materials with food drive to feed the hungry.

"Fullerton Offers Amnesty to Patrons with Overdues." *Library Journal* 110 (October 1, 1985): 24.

Fullerton (California) amnesty was greatly helped by press coverage. The goal was to clear circulation records before automation, to increase public awareness, and to get the books back so that others could read them.

Milner, Art. "Forgiveness Week." *Library Journal* 109 (April 1, 1984): 627–30.

At the Free Library of Philadelphia, a carefully orchestrated and sustained public relations campaign resulted in the return of approximately 160,000 overdues. This is an example of campaign strategy at its best.

"Patrons Give 'Food for Thought' at Milwaukee Public Library." *Library Journal* 114 (February 1, 1989): 23.

The Milwaukee Public Library held an amnesty day dubbed "Food for Thought." Along with getting books back on the shelves, the amnesty day gave patrons a chance to "overcome the guilt" they might feel about possessing an overdue book and return to being regular library users.

Rohr, Judy. "Fine Free Month." *Unabashed Librarian* 52 (1984): 30.

The Fullerton (California) Public Library offered amnesty for one month to borrowers with overdue materials. At the beginning of the month, the library mailed notices to borrowers with long overdue materials. (One of the goals of amnesty was to clear the records before automating.) Press coverage was an important key to their success.

Simpson, T. "Fines for Food: Turning Delinquent Borrowers into Good Samaritans. *Unabashed Librarian* 52 (1884)

Le Mars Public Library in Northwest Iowa decided against a "fine amnesty" as way of inducing people to bring in overdues. An important element was to keep integrity in the fine policy, and one of the biggest barriers seemed to be the punitive nature of fines. The solution: "Fines for Food." People were allowed to contribute to Ethiopian relief in lieu of paying fines. Was it worth it?

STUDIES

Ahiakwo, O. N. and N. P. Obokoh. "Attitudinal Dimension in Library Overdues among Faculty Members—A Case Study." *Library and Information Science Research* 9 (October 1987): 293–304.

Two primary attitudinal factors cause teaching faculty to retain library books longer than allowed. One is "forgetfulness of library obligation over long duration of book use" and the other is "personalization of library materials."

Burgin, Robert. "Guttman Scale Analysis: An Application to Library Science." *Library and Information Science Research* 11 (January 1989): 47–57.

Burgin examines the potential application of Guttman scale analysis to the field of library science. A Guttman scale of restrictiveness is developed dealing with overdues, and data from a 1986 survey of public libraries are fit into the scale.

———— and Patsy Hansel. "Library Overdues: An Update." *Library and Archival Security* 10, no. 2 (1990): 51–75.

The authors present the results of their third study of library strategies to reduce overdue materials.

————. "More Hard Facts on Overdues." *Library and Archival Security* 6, no. 2/3 (summer/fall 1984): 5–18.

This article is based on two surveys (1981 and 1983) of public libraries to determine what tactics employed in the battles against overdues could be statistically validated as effective.

Coady, Reginald P. "Comparing Return Rates of Home Loans of Social Science Material." *Library and Information Science Research* 8 (January 1986): 41–52.

This present study shows a disagreement with earlier research on the return of loans and indicates that the due date may be less important than previously thought in effecting the timely return.

———. "A Comparison of Rates of Return for Home Loans of Natural Science Book Materials." *Collection Management* 8 (spring 1986): 65–78.

This study analyzes the home loan of natural science books for the Ohio State University Libraries. Using the chi square test of association, the return rates of the book materials were compared. It revealed that patron status, subject, penalties, and length of loan period should be further investigated to determine their importance for loan policy.

———. "A Comparison of Single Book Renewals by Subject and Patron Status for Similar Rates of Renewal and Return." *Journal of the American Society for Information Science* 37 (March 1986): 78–85.

A chi square test of equal proportionality is used to compare data sets from a study at Ohio State University. Renewed books are kept longer and consideration for penalties for overdues is suggested.

Farrington, Jean Walter. "Overdues and Academic Libraries: Matters of Access and Collection Control." *Library and Archival Security* 6, no. 2/3 (summer/fall 1984): 67–76.

How overdues are dealt with in an academic library often depends on which group of borrowers is involved. Students, faculty and staff, and outside borrowers all must be treated differently, and there is the potential for serious problems.

Little, Paul. "Managing Overdues: Facts from Four Studies." *Bottom Line* 2, no.2 (1998): 22–5.

A brief summary of two studies on overdues by Robert Burgin and Patsy Hansel on overdues and a study by Jim Broussard, followed by a discussion of the author's study of overdues at the Metropolitan Library System in Oklahoma City.

GENERAL

AL Aside—Oddment: One Humongous Fine." *American Libraries* 25 (February 1994): 139.

A graduate student at the college of Wooster was charged $1,500 in fines for not properly checking books out.

Baxter, Sheila. "In Practice—The Overdue Book Problem." *School Librarian* 37 (February 1989): 14.

The distribution of reminders at South Wilts Grammar School for Girls in Salisbury (England) resulted in a return of 40 percent of overdue books. A progression of follow-up tactics—requesting the books in person to letters and calls to parents—proved effective.

Delgado, J. "Overdue Poem." *Unabashed Librarian* 62 (1987): 20.

A young patron offers to "work off" the fine that she owes the library.

Greenberg, G. "Negligent Borrowers: Readers As Inadvertent Censors." *Ohio Library Association Bulletin* 57 (October 1987): 20–2.

Patrons who do not return library materials are, unwittingly, doing the thing to the collection that censors do intentionally—removing certain materials from the collection so that no other patron can consult them.

"MasterCard and Visa in the Library." *Unabashed Librarian* 65 (1987): 26.

At the Cleveland (Ohio) Public Library overdue fines of $5 or more can be charged with Visa or MasterCard. Photocopies, reproductions of photographs, and reference work contracted from the fee-based Cleveland Research Center can also be charged.

"Overdues." *Unabashed Librarian* 81 (1991): 3–4.

Librarians around Vermont have contributed ideas for getting overdue materials back to the library more quickly.

"Overdues Made Simple." *Unabashed Librarian* 81 (1991): 27.

The Friends of the Davenport (Iowa) Public Library have purpose statement, present a statement concerning overdue procedures.

"Patrons 'Charge It' at Cleveland Public Library. *Library Journal* 112 (November 1, 1987): 24.

Users are delighted with the option to charge their overdues fines at the Cleveland (Ohio) Public Library and their photocopies, reproductions of photographs, and reference work contracted from the fee-based Cleveland Research Center.

Plotnik, Arthur. "Help for the Dun-In Library." *American Libraries* 15 (February 1984): 99.

The author describes the use of a special Library Colletion Service (LCS) which was tested at San Bernardino (California) County Library.

Southards, K. "Checkin' It in." *School Librarian's Workshop* 10 (April 1990): 4–5.

A week-long festival was held to minimize the amount of time spent tracking down missing items.

Sternberg, I. "Amnesty Month: Hoping for a Speedy Recovery." *Unabashed Librarian* 83 (1992): 31.

Listed here are some of the best excuses for why books are late or lost and a collection of unusual items found in books, presumably having served as bookmarks.

INDEX

ABOUT THE EDITOR AND THE AUTHORS

Patsy Hansel is director of the Williamsburg Regional Library in Virginia. She received a master's in history from Wake Forest University, Winston-Salem, North Carolina, and an M.L.S. from the University of North Carolina at Chapel Hill. She is a past president of the North Carolina Library Association and the Virginia Public Library Directors Association. In 1997 she was named Virginia's first Public Library Director of the Year.

Henry Dutcher is presently the supervisor of Borrower's Services for the Springfield (Massachusetts) Library. He received his Master of Library and Information Science degree from the University of Texas at Austin. He has previously held positions at Springfield (Massachusetts) College; Asnuntuck Community College, Enfield, Connecticut; and Holyoke (Massachusetts) Community College. Prior to coming to the Springfield Library, he owned the information brokering business INFO, etc. He has also been an adjunct instructor of computer science for two area colleges. His interest in the library profession developed during his days as a student library assistant at the State University of New York at Fredonia.

Judith Fuss was raised in suburban Philadelphia, Pennsylvania, and graduated with a B.S. in social welfare from Pennsylvania State University. Travel around the country and as far away as Japan led finally to Williamsburg, Virginia. After raising her family, she began her work in libraries behind the circulation desk, where she developed programs for training circulation staff. As systems administrator, she oversees the operation of Williamsburg's automated library system, including the electronic notification system, and administers the library's participation in the setoff debt collection program.

Jeff Hall is operations manager at Rowan Public Library, Salisbury, North Carolina, where he has worked for the past ten years. He received his master's degree in library science at the University of North Carolina at Greensboro. He has been a frequent speaker on the use of technology in libraries. He has spoken at the Computers in Libraries Conference, at the State Library of South Carolina Internet Conference, and at individual library staff development programs. He also has served as a consultant for planning and implementing automated library systems and local area networks.

Melody Moxley is administrative services manager at Rowan Public Library, Salisbury, North Carolina. She received her undergraduate degree at Lenoir-Rhyne College, Hickory, North Carolina, and her M.S.L.S. at the University of Tennessee. She is an audiovisual reviewer for *AudioFile, Kliatt, Library Journal,* and *School Library Journal.* She has also published articles in *American Libraries* and *North Carolina Libraries,* and she served as a judge for the Audio Publishers Association's 1998 Audie Awards.

Susan Swanton is library director of the Gates Public Library, which is in the town of Gates, New York, outside of Rochester. She has held this position since 1965. She has a B.A. in American history from Harvard and an M.L.S. from Columbia University. She is a past president of the Gates-Chili Council of the Rochester Chamber of Commerce and in 1994 was named citizen of the year. She is also a past president of the Rochester Drug and Alcohol Council.

Sharon Winters is deputy director for support services at Pierce County Library in Tacoma, Washington. She wrote this article during her tenure as support services manager at Hampton (Virginia) Public Library. Winters served as president of CODI, the Dynix/Ameritech national users group, in 1995-96 and was part-time lecturer for Catholic University's Library and Information Science program while in Virginia. She holds an M.L.S. from the University of North Carolina at Greensboro and an M.P.A. from George Washington University, Washington, D.C.

Susan M. Johns is currently associate professor of library science at Pittsburg (Kansas) State University and has served as head of systems and head of circulation at the Axe Library (Pittsburg, Kansas) since 1987. She graduated with a B.A. in English and Music in 1979 from Southwestern College, Winfield, Kansas, and received an M.S. in library and information science from the University of Illinois Urbana–Champaign in 1987. She is active in regional and state library organizations and serves as president of CODI (1998), the Dynix/Ameritech National Users' group. Her research interests include techniques for beta-testing of software and various facets of internationalization in software design.

Julie Walker received her B.A. in political science and a Master of Science in Library Science from the University of North Carolina at Chapel Hill. She has held reference and branch-manager positions in Winston-Salem, Asheboro, and Charlotte, North Carolina. She is currently assistant director of the Athens Regional Library System in Athens, Georgia. She is also an automation consultant for public libraries and the associate editor of *The Georgia Librarian.*

Terry B. Prather earned a Master of Library Science from North Carolina Central University in Durham. She has been a reference librarian for fifteen years, serving libraries in Perquimans and Davidson Counties in North Carolina. She is currently reference librarian at the Charles A. Cannon Memorial Library, Kannapolis (North Carolina) Branch.